The Unscripted Classroom

Also from Susan Stacey

Emergent Curriculum in Early Childhood Settings: From Theory to Practice

The Unscripted Classroom

Emergent Curriculum in Action

Susan Stacey

Redleaf Press®
www.redleafpress.org
800-423-8309

Published by Redleaf Press
10 Yorkton Court
St. Paul, MN 55117
www.redleafpress.org

First edition 2011
Cover design by Jim Handrigan
Cover photograph © Blend Images Photography/Veer
Interior typeset in Garamond and MrsEaves and designed by Jim Handrigan
Printed in the United States of America
18 17 16 15 14 13 12 11   1 2 3 4 5 6 7 8

Library of Congress Cataloging-in-Publication Data
Stacey, Susan.
    The unscripted classroom : emergent curriculum in action / Susan Stacey.
       p. cm.
    Includes bibliographical references.
    ISBN 978-1-60554-036-8 (pbk.)
    1. Early childhood education—Curricula. 2. Creative teaching. 3. Student-centered learning. 4. Observation (Educational method) 5. Lesson planning.   I. Title.
LB1139.4.S74 2011
372.19—dc22

                                        2010048537

Printed on acid-free paper

9/2/11

For Alexander, Joseph, and Eva

Contents

Acknowledgments

This book would not be in your hands without the teachers, administrators, and teacher educators who agreed to share their stories: Donna Stapleton, Lana O'Reilly, Anne Marie Coughlin, Melissa Pinkham, Susan Hagner, Michelle Tessier, Liz Rogers, Andrea Foster, Shannon Harrison, Lori Warner, Hope Moffatt, Karyn Callaghan, and Naomi Robinson. All of these women are involved in education in ways above and beyond their inspired classroom work. They nurture our profession by thinking deeply and by advocating for excellence in teaching. They read with endless curiosity, attend meetings, and belong to professional organizations. On top of all this, they also lead busy lives as mothers, partners, and involved community members. Their hectic pace only makes their generosity more noteworthy. I thank each of them for taking the time to talk with me, answer endless e-mail requests, and hunt down photographs to enrich this work.

Carol Anne Wien offered support and encouragement when I was puzzled or stuck. There are many others to whom I owe a great debt for provoking my thinking about early education. They know who they are. In particular, I want to thank three Elizabeths: Liz Rogers, Liz Hicks, and Elizabeth Jones—provocateurs with whom I am able to try out new ideas and clarify my thinking.

Elizabeth (Betty) Jones recently retired from full-time college teaching, and I would like to take this opportunity to thank her for her lifetime of work in the field. The value of her thinking, writing, and teaching—always with warmth, honesty, and humor—is immeasurable. Thank you, Betty, from all of us.

Introduction

As an educator, you find solutions and make decisions every day, all day long. You sometimes think on your feet, responding in the moment to what is happening during play, to a question a child asks, or to an observation that prompts you to provide support for the child. At other times, you carry out planned activities. How do you decide what to plan? How does your decision making unfold? Do you follow activities planned by other people, or do you respond to events with activities you feel are just right for a particular group of children at a particular time?

Emergent curriculum can be defined as a cycle that involves

- watching and listening to children with care;

- reflecting on and engaging in dialogue with others about what is happening; and

- responding thoughtfully in ways that support children's ideas, questions, and thinking.

In an emergent curriculum setting, a teacher's response to children needs to be original because children's ideas are often unexpected, thought-provoking, or just plain puzzling. More traditional and prescriptive curriculum books cannot provide teachers with a script for what to do next in response to children. Teachers who use emergent curriculum must think creatively to keep children's thinking at the forefront of the curriculum while also remaining accountable to parents, administrators, and professional guidelines in the field.

Emergent curriculum can be implemented with children of all ages. Teachers who use emergent curriculum are keen observers and listeners. These qualities serve every age group well. By closely observing nonverbal toddlers, listening to a heated discussion among preschoolers, or responding to first graders' ideas, teachers are giving children what they deserve. All children deserve recognition of their competence and reassurance that their ideas and actions have value in the world.

Many teachers are enthusiastic about emergent curriculum because the approach offers choices for the children and themselves as well as the chance to respond to children in creative ways. Teachers and children benefit when children have opportunities to be fully engaged in *their* explorations, *their* topics, or *their* ideas.

Throughout my career, I have worked extensively with student teachers, beginning teachers, and seasoned practitioners. When first introduced to emergent curriculum, they each have similar questions: What am I looking for when I observe? How will I know what to do next? How do I keep my responses original and attuned to the children? How do I meet the standards required by the organization? And, there is one question they ask most frequently: With so many tangents during children's play, how do I choose what to focus on?

Learning from Stories

One of the most valuable ways to learn about teaching is to watch others at work and engage in dialogue with them about why they do what they do in a particular way. This book is based on stories from teachers who shared experiences from their own classrooms. In particular, there is a focus on *how* they made decisions, or what led them to do what they did. By understanding their creative thinking, hopefully you will be inspired to step outside your usual scripts and try something that feels new to you, that links observations to curriculum, that creates passion for your work, and that leads to innovative practices within your classroom. Such practices originate with collaboration between the children and their teachers.

How This Book Works

Chapter 1 begins with a review of what emergent curriculum is and what it is not, establishing a shared understanding and vocabulary. The role of observation and listening is presented, and an example of emergent curriculum—a story titled "The E-mail Project"—is included as well. A short conversation from the e-mail project is analyzed for information on decision making, group work with children, and time frames.

Chapter 2 examines creativity. What is creativity? What does it look like in everyday teaching practice? This chapter examines the value of dialogue, the director's role, the physical environment, and the children's use of materials within the environment. The story of Zi Hao and his teacher illustrates the teacher's struggles and successes as she tries to collaborate with him in a creative way to understand dinosaur skeletons.

In chapter 3, the importance and benefits of teachers telling stories is explained. As an example, the staff of one organization shared their teaching stories as a means of professional development. Two stories from the teachers exemplify emergent practices and teacher reflection.

Chapters 4 through 8 are devoted to teachers' stories. These examples of classroom practice are all different yet linked by the creative and flexible ways the teachers responded to a challenge or to the children's ideas. The stories include many possibilities for responding to ideas and events, including

- developing further provocations and activities;

- scaffolding the child's knowledge;

- making changes in the physical environment;

- using documentation as a tool for reflection;

- following unexpected tangents; and

- writing a plan for a curriculum that emerges.

Chapter 9 presents the role of teacher education programs and their influence on the future of the education of young children. Current teaching and learning about emergent curriculum, as well as the challenges, are examined. The role of the administrator is also discussed, since often an administrator's leadership determines the success of any curriculum path. What types of skills does an administrator need? What kinds of support must be offered for staff?

Finally, chapter 10 examines a project that brings together all aspects of emergent curriculum from the perspective of a teacher who is very new to and unsure about this approach. What creative responses were involved? How did it feel for that teacher? This chapter also explores what you can do now. It is always wise to have a goal in mind when engaging in new practices or enriching a present approach. To provide you with a starting point, ideas and resources to ponder are included in this chapter.

The bibliography includes cited works and suggested readings to expand and support your work and your thinking. Some of these resources may take you outside your area of expertise, which is intentional. When we read about types of work unrelated to our own profession, we often gain insight into our own field or discover a new way of thinking.

Introducing Naomi

Naomi is a real person. She is a teacher who has worked with the preschool age group and with emergent curriculum for only one year. Although familiar with the theories surrounding emergent curriculum, Naomi felt both excited and lost when she was asked to move from a first grade to a prekindergarten classroom. She was excited to grow and to learn more about this approach, but she felt lost because it was so different from anything she had tried before.

Naomi kept a teaching journal during her first year in the prekindergarten class. She recorded her successes, her questions, and her disequilibrium. As noted earlier, it is important for teachers to share their stories, and Naomi generously agreed to share some of her thoughts from her new adventure. Throughout this book, snippets of Naomi's journal that relate to the topic being discussed are included. Hopefully these journal entries will be reassuring for teachers; I expect some readers will recognize themselves in her writing!

When a teacher steps out of his or her comfort zone, as Naomi did, a window opens. By expanding on our prior knowledge and by thinking creatively, we can attempt to have original responses or to try new approaches. Creativity in teaching offers young children stimulation, engagement, passion, and a love of learning. It also offers opportunities to refresh our teaching, to take a new look at what our teaching practices are, and to examine the *why* in our teaching.

1

Revisiting Emergent Curriculum

The teacher neither brings the curriculum to the school nor is he or she solely the creator of such. Rather, the teacher is only one of the contributors to the creation of the relationship they call "school."

—CAROL BRUNSON DAY

Emergent curriculum allows teachers to collaborate with children around their ideas, questions, development, and topics of interest. It is a continuous cycle that requires teachers to observe children and to listen closely for their ideas. Observation and listening are followed by the teacher's thoughtful response, which builds on what the children are doing and thinking. These thoughtful responses come about through discussion among the teaching team. Teachers may ask themselves, "What are the children really trying to understand?" "What developmental task is underlying this exploration?" or "How is this child trying to figure out how this works?" These questions lead teachers to reflect on what might happen next, how to proceed, or what to look for in subsequent observations.

*Continued observation and formulation of questions.

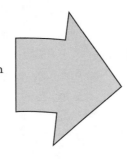

Reflecting with others on observations, experiences, and narratives.

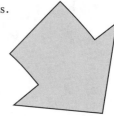

What intrigues or puzzles me? What do I wonder?

Next steps?

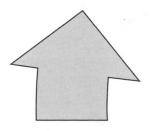

A Continuous Cycle

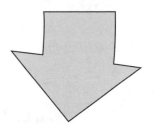

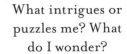

Specifically, what are the children trying to find out?

How are the children responding?

What does it all mean? Search for patterns or insights.

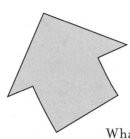

What do we offer as an invitation? As support? In terms of exploration?

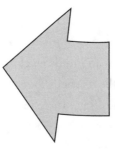

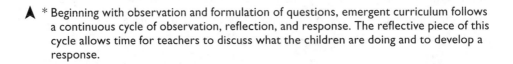

▲ * Beginning with observation and formulation of questions, emergent curriculum follows a continuous cycle of observation, reflection, and response. The reflective piece of this cycle allows time for teachers to discuss what the children are doing and to develop a response.

Emergent curriculum is not a new approach, but it may feel unfamiliar to many early childhood and elementary school practitioners. Depending on your training, you may have learned about themes or units with set time frames that teachers decide on. Or perhaps you learned to approach curriculum planning with a developmental lens, thinking "If the majority of children are at this age or stage, we should be doing this." You may be a part of an organization in which terms such as *outcomes, goals,* or *benchmarks* are used. While developmentally appropriate curricula might have been written with specific developmental goals in mind, we must be mindful of how these goals or outcomes are responsive to individual children. It is important to consider the children's interests, questions, prior knowledge, and cultures.

Throughout this book, the term *project* refers to either long-term (weeks or months) or short-term (days) work on a topic of interest. By collaborating with children and scaffolding their learning, teachers can make projects in-depth rather than superficial. For example, a study of birds might last only a few days if the birds are the only topic of study; whereas, if teachers are able to provoke the children's interest in habitats, trees, nest building, bird communication, and so on, then the project delves much further into the whole world of birds and becomes a deep investigation.

Inquiry is another term associated with emergent curriculum. Inquiry is a repeating cycle that might begin with a question or theory from children or with an observation of children by teachers. After reflection, teachers provide invitations (such as preliminary activities or materials) to ascertain the depth of interest. Then, they observe what happens. If the topic continues to capture the children's interest, teachers will continue to provide invitations, engage in conversations with children, observe, and reflect again. A continuous cycle of inquiry allows all participants—adults and children—to dig deeper into the topic and to veer off into related topics if warranted.

Naomi's Journal

I'm finding myself pretty overwhelmed in these early days. I am struggling to readjust to this age group and what is developmentally appropriate for them. Everything is new and exciting to me, and sometimes I am feeling overstimulated because I don't know what to focus on/attend to. I would imagine the children often find themselves feeling similarly. If so, then I should be sure to keep things simple in the beginning and start with just a few materials. On the

*bright side, I am feeling challenged in a positive way. I think that as the year
rolls on I will find my footing in a less clumsy manner.*

Misunderstandings and Questions

Responsible educators always keep all areas of children's development—physical,
cognitive, fine and gross motor, language and communication, and social and
emotional—in mind when planning quality programs. Some common misunderstandings about emergent curriculum are found in academic learning. The most frequently asked questions about merging emergent curriculum and children's learning
about language, literacy, mathematics, and science concepts follow.

Is all of the curriculum emergent all the time? It depends on how one defines
curriculum! If "curriculum is what happens," as Laura Dittmann (1970, 1) suggests,
then everything children do is fodder for curriculum development. If this question
refers to in-depth projects, then no—projects are not happening all the time. Sometimes, between strong interests about how something works or ideas pertaining
to children's experiences, there are periods when the classroom ticks nicely along.
Children explore materials, learn how to be in a group, form relationships, play out
scenarios from home, and do all the other thousands of things that children do in
early childhood settings, while teachers watch and listen carefully so they are ready
to respond to children's interests and questions.

What happens to academics in an emergent curriculum classroom? It
would be irresponsible to ignore the signs children give us when they are ready to
learn about something. We watch for these cues all the time. For example, we might
hear children asking questions about print, see them experiment with forming it,
read it from predictable books, and recognize it within the environment. In any
setting, including one that uses emergent curriculum, we respond to such cues by
providing *developmentally appropriate* opportunities to use print in meaningful
ways. Carol Copple and Sue Bredekamp's work *Developmentally Appropriate Practice in Early Childhood Programs Serving Children from Birth through Age 8* (2009)
outlines what these developmentally appropriate opportunities look like. Whether
or not children are engaged in an inquiry or a long-term project, developmentally
appropriate invitations, classroom work areas, and opportunities still exist.

It is, in fact, easier to incorporate print, math, or science concepts into an investigation that is intensely engaging for the children because they are then intrinsically motivated to write, draw, and think deeply about their work. Science-based investigations need to be labeled and explained, research through reading has to be done around unfamiliar topics, numbers and graphing have to be used within some projects, and so on. All of this is meaningful work and, therefore, engaging as well as academic in nature.

What about assessment? Documentation, which is addressed throughout this book, is an excellent way for teachers to assess what children know, how deeply they understand, and what their needs are. The child's portfolio is one form of documentation that is particularly useful when discussing children's progress with their parents. Easy to develop, the portfolio provides an in-depth look at individual children.

If we keep in mind that children are fully engaged when they are truly interested in a topic, then the idea of watching and listening to children in order to uncover those topics makes perfect sense. How can teachers possibly choose topics for investigation weeks or months in advance? Children develop at a rapid rate, thinking of ideas and questions teachers could never have anticipated. At a very young age, children are also able to come up with theories about how the world works. Children's theories need to be taken seriously and should be addressed by exploring their thinking and supporting the work that will scaffold their learning about topics of interest to them.

Using emergent curriculum, educators work alongside children as coconstructors of knowledge, paying close attention to the children's thinking and questions. When children's ideas and topics are unexpected or puzzling to teachers, it should be fun for teachers to develop curriculum and learn with the children. The added excitement helps to keep work enjoyable. Rather than being entrenched in familiar topics of early childhood programs, such as transportation, seasons, or families, you may instead find yourself exploring e-mail, inukshuk, lines, quilts, or statues! These more unusual investigations (all of which I have experienced with children) are unlikely to be found in prescriptive curriculum manuals that lay out activities to do and questions to ask. The teaching team will need to discuss children's ideas and respond to them in innovative ways.

Naomi's Journal

I have really been enjoying the process of learning to observe closely and document carefully. I see now that, as a teacher, there are many moments I have probably missed in the past that really show just what a child does and does not know and is/isn't interested in. I feel like I am already becoming a slightly better "reader" of children and perhaps myself.

My Story: The E-mail Project

The emergent curriculum cycle begins with observation and listening. Teachers should listen to children's explicit ideas and uncover what is under the surface of what they are saying. Observation and listening will probably raise some questions for teachers: What do the children mean? How did they come to that conclusion or idea? What is their prior knowledge in this area? How can we find out more about their understanding?

Three- to five-year-olds can often express their reasoning—why they think what they think, or what they know about something—when there is an attentive and interested listener. The listener must be able to maintain a conversation with the child and ask authentic questions. A true conversation, which requires give and take, enables both participants to gather information as well as to offer it.

Within my own classroom of four- and five-year-olds at the Halifax Grammar School in Halifax, Nova Scotia, an opportunity came up for children to have a conversation about e-mail. We did not begin on this topic but on the more familiar topic of regular mail. The children previously built their own mailbox, and we were discussing how mail works. It occurred to me during this conversation that these children probably knew something about electronic mail, and I wanted to explore this idea further.

> TEACHER: Is there another way of sending mail?
> ALEXANDER: Yes! E-mail. My mom does that!
> TEACHER: How does e-mail work?
> ALEXANDER: It has words . . . it goes in the mailbox.
> NOOR: No! It's something that goes in the printer!
> AUSTIN: Yes . . . you use the things . . . (imitates typing with his hands).

> NOOR: It's in the computer and a square comes. You do something with the arrow and it comes out on the printer.
>
> TEACHER: Ah . . . so it's faster than regular mail?
>
> NOOR: E-mail goes faster (everyone nods in agreement).
>
> LIAM: You just press the button and it says "Open Sesame!"

This three-minute conversation provides a wealth of information about the children's prior knowledge and understanding. My question, "How does e-mail work?" is an authentic question in that I don't know the answer to it. Therefore, I'm not testing the children or looking for a correct answer. I had (and still have) little understanding about the details of how e-mail really works, and I was trying to uncover the children's ideas about this mysterious form of communication that is a common part of all our lives.

The question is also hard to answer. The concept of e-mail communication is difficult to wrap one's mind around and difficult to explain. This type of question may not usually be asked of young children. But our colleagues in Reggio Emilia, Italy, have taught us, among other things, to trust in the competence of the child. We should not underestimate children's willingness to try to explain things that are difficult to understand. Usually, children will give it a try, and they often think out loud. This is beneficial because it opens up the opportunity for other children to chime in and for the teacher to get a glimpse of their thinking.

The first child's response shows some confusion. He knows that e-mail has words but mentions the conventional mailbox. Noor chimes in to try to correct this notion and, also, adds the idea of words going into the printer. When the teaching team thought together about this comment, it was puzzling at first and then completely understandable. The manifestation of e-mail— what the child sees in concrete terms—is often a printout of the e-mail message that comes out of the printer.

Collaborating on a Theory of Email....

During a discussion about regular mail (Nov 20), the following conversation occurred:

Ms. Stacey:	Is there another way to send mail?
Alexander:	Yes! Email....my mom does that.
Ms. Stacey:	How does email work?
Alexander:	It has words. It goes in the mailbox.
Noor:	No! It's something that goes in the printer...
Austin:	Yes...you use the things (makes typing motion with hands)
Noor:	It's in the computer, and a square comes. You do something with the arrow, and it comes out – on the printer.
Ms. Stacey:	Which is faster, email or regular mail?
Noor:	Email goes faster.
Liam:	You just press the button, and it says 'Open Sesame!'

Reflecting on this conversation, we could see some prior knowledge and experience with seeing the physical manifestation of email: The computer, the keyboard, clicking to send, and the printer printing out the message. However, we wondered if the children could go a step further and express ideas about how the email arrived at its destination.

▲ The first page of documentation for the e-mail project.

The next child, unable to think of the word for keyboard, instead uses his hands to mimic fingers on a keyboard, which explains the process of typing an e-mail message.

Noor's final comment demonstrates her familiarity with what actually happens on the screen: The e-mail is, according to Noor, "in the computer." A "square comes," which the teaching group took to mean the window appears on the screen. You "do something with the arrow," which probably refers to a mouse click and the cursor, and "it comes out on the printer!" Noor's final comment proves, to her, that e-mail does indeed come out of the printer.

In the last comment from Liam, we see a lovely connection between the world of technology and the world of classic literature. "Open Sesame" are the magic words from *Ali Baba and the Forty Thieves*. It surely must seem magical to a child when an adult clicks on a window on the computer screen and a message appears.

From this brief example, we can see the importance of paying attention to children's ideas, asking authentic questions, and then, through reflection, trying to interpret the response. This reflection and interpretation, which I refer to in my first book, *Emergent Curriculum in Early Childhood Settings*, as the "missing middle," is sometimes missing when observations and conversations are linked to a curriculum plan. Teachers are a busy, multitasking group, and we tend to be efficient and speedy in coming up with a plan for how to respond to children. I suggest we take the time to stop and think, for a few days if necessary, before proceeding. Teams of teachers should discuss children's ideas and reflect on what their actions or words communicate about their understandings or misunderstandings. Only then should we proceed to make a plan for what to do next. In the case of the e-mail conversation, for example, it took a few days to decide whether this topic was worth pursuing.

How do teachers decide what to pursue? We see and hear dozens of ideas and possibilities from children every day. How do we decide which ideas to follow and what to do?

Decision Making in Emergent Curriculum

When we work with children over a long period of time, we know them well. We know what is new for children and what is familiar. We know their developmental stages, interests, strengths, and challenges. We are in relationships with these children. We think with them, joke with them, and have many conversations. Knowing children is the bedrock for building curriculum *for a particular group of children*.

If you suspect a topic may be worth investigating, it is useful to slow down and watch further. You might ask yourself the following questions:

- How many children are involved? The children's interests might be followed individually or in small or large groups.

- Are they asking questions about the topic and, perhaps, trying to move forward by themselves? It is important to pay attention to the children's questions in order to know which tangents of an inquiry to follow. A large topic (such as oceans) has many possibilities for investigation, and the children's questions will help guide you.

- What are they saying in conversations with each other? These conversations will often tell us about what the children really understand or misunderstand.

- Are they acting out scenarios during play that connect with an idea? Play is a language that explains the children's thinking and ideas. What do we see in these scenarios? Can we act on what we see?

- Do they continue to circle back to the topic even when other things are going on in the classroom? Their persistence sends a message that this topic is, indeed, of great interest.

It is important to note that it is rare for all children to be engaged in the same investigation at the same time. Often there are multiple agendas within a group, with small groups of children pursuing different interests.

It is also key to think about your understanding of the topic. If you do not know much about the area of interest, will it be easy for you to find out more? Can you bring in someone else to share his or her expertise? Does your larger community have resources to support the investigation? In other words, can *you* learn in collaboration with the children?

Groups and Time Frames

Since most early childhood educators work in teams, it is possible for each adult to take responsibility for supporting different topics of interest. One teacher, for example, might follow a group of six children who are developing an idea for building a machine. Another teacher might work with children who are experimenting with color and lines. If there is a third member on the team, this teacher may take care of more general work going on in the classroom by moving from one area to another,

The documentation of the e-mail project continues and includes children's ideas and drawings as well as photos of children at work.

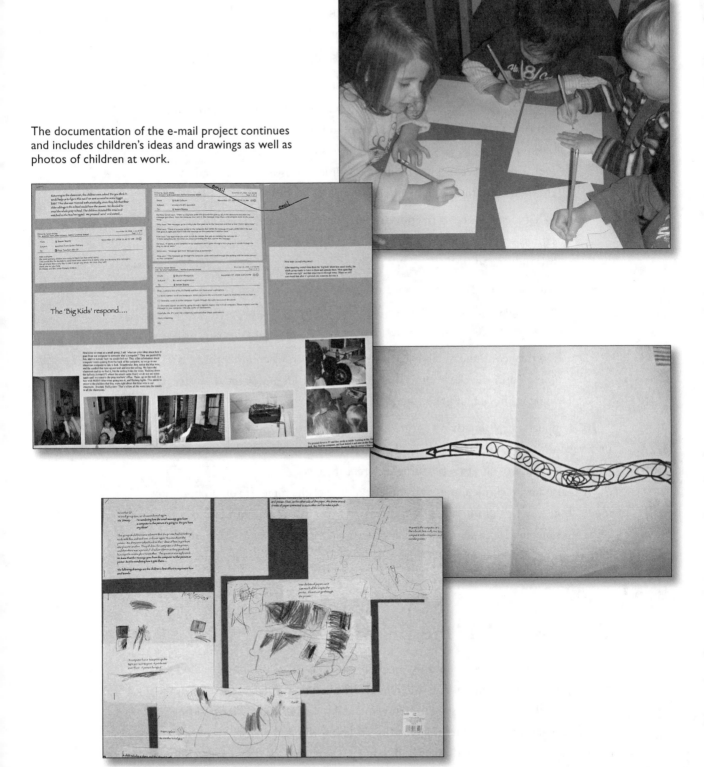

perhaps supporting children in the reading or construction areas. The e-mail project is an example of how each teacher supports a different topic of interest.

Six children were present for the original conversation. Some were contributing ideas, and some were listening. These six children continued to talk about e-mail for the next couple of days, and they noticed when I was using the classroom computer to send e-mail. Since our classroom had small-group times as part of the daily routine, it was easy for me to embark on an investigation of e-mail with this small group of children. My teaching partner, Martine, worked with the other children to meet their developmental needs using their areas of interest.

For these six children, their work on investigating e-mail lasted two weeks. They thought that e-mail had something to do with the wires coming from the computer and that the words traveled through the wires. Over the course of two weeks, we followed the wires around the school, e-mailed older children in the school to solicit their ideas about how e-mail works (and received some very complex responses even the teachers did not understand), and drew ideas.

The work was documented, and when e-mail was mentioned again months later, the children were able to refer to the documentation and revisit their original thoughts. This small group of children was the only group that became interested in e-mail.

When an idea really excites and engages a small group of children, it is common for other children to eventually join them. There is something contagious about a good idea, and other children will often add their own thoughts to enrich the project. When this happens, ideas may be shared during class meeting (circle) times. When many children are talking, it is helpful to have another teacher nearby to act as a scribe. The scribe writes down the children's words so the teacher working directly with the children is free to really listen and think about what the children are saying. Alternatively, you may wish to use a digital recorder. This is particularly useful when working alone or at times when the teaching team would like to listen to the conversation at a later time.

In some classrooms, depending on how the day is organized, teachers provide a specific time for group investigations, such as small-group time. This can work well, as long as the time provided is lengthy and flexible and the environment is well provisioned with materials for independent work outside of group times so children can continue to experiment and investigate throughout the day. For example, the studio/art area should contain many ways for the children to represent what they know or are interested in as opportunities arise.

Continuing the Cycle

When an idea arises and when children and teachers want to pursue the work further, it is essential to provide materials to work with and space that is well provisioned for exploration. Supporters, such as teachers and older children or visitors, as well as activities designed to help children construct further knowledge about their topic are also essential. Throughout all of these offerings and investigations, it is also important to continue watching and listening. More ideas will occur, and we need to be attentive to new thoughts the children express, questions that come up, and the inevitable tangents that will evolve. These questions and conversations will move the project forward. In other words, the work and the children themselves provide the answers to questions, such as "What to do next?" "What are the children wondering about?" "What are the teachers' questions about the children's work" and "How can the teachers find the answers?"

As various aspects of emergent curriculum are addressed in this book, the way other teachers have worked through this process is uncovered. There are side references on some pages that link what is happening in the text to a particular aspect of emergent curriculum. Naomi's reflections about these aspects are included, as she works in an emergent setting for the first time, providing some insight into how it feels to be unfamiliar with the approach.

Rather than seeing a neat and tidy list of what to do and when to do it, hopefully you will instead see the spiraling nature of emergent curriculum. For teachers and children in a responsive classroom, one thing leads to another. A child's idea leads to reflective dialogue between teachers and perhaps an invitation to an activity, which leads to more questions for the teachers. There are rarely straight lines from A to B in emergent curriculum, and that is what makes it so exciting, stimulating, and thought provoking. It is also what makes creativity an important aspect of emergent curriculum. The next chapter presents how creativity and emergent curriculum are linked.

Creative Thinking in Emergent Curriculum

I would suggest that creativity is a mind that is fresh, alert, sensitive. It is a mind that is not dull, mechanical, afraid, restricted. Creativity is an energy which moves through the whole body. Creativity can simply be seeing each day as new and fresh and full of potential.

—F. David Peat

When asked "What is creativity?" many people immediately think about the graphic or performing arts. Painters, sculptors, musicians, actors, or designers may spring to mind.

Creativity extends much further than the arts. Throughout time, creative thinkers, including scientists, artists, and philosophers, have moved societies to think in alternate ways, discover diverse techniques and approaches, and solve problems or develop something new and exciting. But society rarely acknowledges the creativity involved in mathematics, science, or research.

When trying to define *creativity* in words, it becomes clear that there are widely different opinions of what it is, what it looks and feels like, and how one knows when it is present. Our reading and experiences may tell us that creativity involves original thinking, innovation, or making connections. So when we think about creative teachers, what is it that springs to mind?

Scholars, such as Mihaly Csikszentmihalyi, Howard Gardner, Sir Ken Robinson, and many others, have done a great deal of thinking and writing about creativity. Robinson (2009), when referring to creativity and the lack of it within education, raises an interesting point: Since we do not know what the world will look like in twenty years, when today's young children will be adults in the workforce, how can we possibly know what to teach them? The answer, of course, is that teaching facts that will quickly become obsolete is of no use. Rather, we must empower children to learn how to learn and to enjoy the process. Children will also need many chances to construct their own knowledge. Knowing how to investigate and think is a powerful tool that will stay with them forever. And if they become creative thinkers, they will have the potential to discover previously unknown paths.

What kind of learning climate sets the stage for children and teachers to think creatively together? What supports must be present for all of the learners? What role does ambience play? And what will this setting look and feel like in real life? To answer these questions, we must examine the value of dialogue, the physical environment, and the multiple ways of expressing ideas.

The Value of Dialogue with Other Adults

Teachers who respond creatively to children often say they rarely come up with wonderful ideas when they are thinking alone. When teachers talk, referring to reflective dialogue rather than planning, they bounce ideas off each other, brainstorming their way toward thinking outside the box.

There is something to remember about brainstorming. As designer Kathy Kaulbach (2010, pers. comm.) points out, "We have to be brainstorming with the right set of people who are willing to go into uncharted waters and build. There is no ego trip involved here. We have to be willing to really listen to others' ideas and consider them." When you have experienced the excitement of an aha moment, you then understand the power of thinking together and, as Eleanor Duckworth (2006, 1) says, "the having of wonderful ideas." For example, you might share a puzzling play scenario or a child's question in discussion among teachers. Those events that made you feel stuck may suddenly become clearer when you hear others' points of view. Others may suggest a path that had not occurred to you. It is always enlightening to hear others' perspectives when struggling with an intriguing situation.

Alternatively, you may be conversing with someone who has no relationship to your profession. But in listening to them speak about their own work, you suddenly make a connection to yours. This has happened to me many times, especially when speaking with close friends. I do not profess to have enough knowledge about the brain to explain how this happens. I just know when I hear others talk about a book, idea, or experience, sometimes a window seems to open in my mind and I am able to connect their thinking with my own work. This experience is a mystery to me, but it's one I have come to value. I believe that this capacity to relate to others' experiences has something to do with our *openness* to possible connections. We use the term *open mind* quite loosely in our society, but when it comes to our work, we teachers can be quite scripted rather than open. Instead, we should remain open to alternate ways of doing *anything* that is a part of our day with children.

Naomi's Journal

Today I had an interesting conversation with a colleague who was my grade partner when I taught grade one last year. She was picking my brain about emergent curriculum, and although I didn't feel equipped to answer all of her questions, thinking about them helped me to answer some of my own.

A DIRECTOR'S CONTRIBUTION

Donna Stapleton, the director of Small World Learning Centre in Bridgewater, Nova Scotia, has worked hard to provide teachers with time for open thinking and discussion. She understands that dialogue assists teachers in the process of thinking about what to do next in response to what children are doing and saying. Like most early childhood directors, she works within a tight budget that does not allow the luxury of substitutes during meeting times or overtime pay for meeting after work. So Donna decided to change the nature of the center's regular staff meetings, which are held once a month. Instead of dealing with business and routine items, staff meetings are devoted to teachers sharing their work and talking about it in depth.

Donna linked this sharing time to the study of emergent curriculum. The staff read a chapter of *Emergent Curriculum in Early Childhood Settings* (Stacey 2009) each month. Then they explored and experimented within their classrooms using the concepts they studied. During staff meetings, they discussed what happened as a result of these explorations. This study-group type of reflective dialogue encourages teachers to link theory to practice. Teachers are encouraged to articulate to others what happened, what it means, and what they will try next. Donna describes this process below.

> Each teaching team has an initial ten-minute block to describe what they did in their classrooms and what they think might happen next. They talk about things like "What did we learn?" and "What else can we try?" It's exciting to see teachers making connections they might not have made if they weren't involved in this kind of reading and dialogue. There are many types of personalities involved, such as people who don't like to speak up in a group and people who talk too much. Everyone is given time to speak, and we follow up with discussion. I think some of the quieter people process the conversations on their own time and come back with good ideas a few days later. Sometimes I think these more introverted personalities are actually extremely reflective since they take the time to really process information before responding.
>
> We have a parent who supports us in this process by providing food for us, so we have supper together as we talk. And we use a large sand timer so those who are talking can see it and keep within their time frame. We don't have unlimited time. These are evening meetings, and everyone has a family to go to or is just plain tired. We want to give everyone a chance to speak. For some people, ten minutes seems like a very long time, and for others it goes really quickly. People listen intently to each other, and we often experience aha moments as something suddenly becomes clear. When teachers see their colleagues become really excited about their work, they begin to see the value of their own work too. This helps them recall moments they may previously have overlooked.
>
> Another way we learn about our colleagues' work is to occasionally take time to switch places and work in each other's rooms for a day or two. When you are a newcomer to a room, you see things with fresh eyes and can offer really meaningful input about things the teacher might not have noticed.

Most early childhood centers hold regular staff meetings, but often these gatherings become entrenched in old scripts of updates, news, policies, problem issues, and so on. Since Donna's staff members are working hard to embrace emergent curriculum and are short on time and money for meetings, she found a more creative and valuable way to use their time.

Donna reports that a huge percentage of news and business is handled through written communication in the staff room or, for smaller matters, by simply touching base during the day. No one seems to miss dealing with these issues together at meetings, and the organization continues to run efficiently.

It is important to note that this center has placed value on sharing, experimentation, and study. Creativity is a process. In *The Element*, Ken Robinson (2009, 71–72) describes what this might look like: "The creative process begins with an inkling . . . which requires further development. This is a journey that can have many different phases and unexpected turns; it can draw on different sorts of skills and knowledge and end up somewhere entirely unpredicted at the outset. . . . Creativity involves several different processes that wind through each other. The first is generating new ideas, imagining different possibilities, considering alternative options."

When Donna decided to change the way staff meetings were run, she was imagining a different possibility, and her staff benefited. They now have the option to think together about their inklings and use their varied skill sets and knowledge to think about even more possibilities for the children in their care and for their own research.

The Classroom as a Workshop for Ideas

When thinking about relationships, we tend to focus on relationships with people. As educators, we regularly consider relationship building in our work with young children. Children also have a relationship with their physical environment. How the classroom environment evolves and functions sends a clear message about our own values and philosophies and directly affects how children respond to it. If we want our classrooms to be a workshop for ideas about how the world works and our own role within it, then we have to think about how we might support creative thinking when we design our rooms.

What kind of rooms and spaces provide an ideal atmosphere for creative thinking? We all respond differently to different kinds of environments, depending on our dispositions. You may find you concentrate more intensely in a silent room, while your colleague needs noise in the background. For some people, natural light and aesthetically beautiful environments are a catalyst for creativity, while others prefer the subdued lighting of a cozy study or to work in the outdoors. In his work *Creativity*, Mihaly Csikszentmihalyi (1996, 146) explains, "At any point in time, what matters most is that we shape the immediate surroundings, activities, and schedules so as to feel in harmony with the small segment of the universe where we happen to be located. . . . The implications for everyday life are simple. . . . There should be room for immersion in concentrated activity and for stimulating novelty. The objects around you should help you become what you intend to be."

This quote reminds me of a friend of mine who is an artist and writer. Norene's studio is full of interesting and whimsical objects. Some she's found outdoors and others she's picked up at various places on her travels. There are pictures clipped from magazines—beautiful vistas, odd designs, intriguing shapes, and everyday things photographed from strange angles. Norene surrounds herself with inspirational artifacts, perhaps, as Csikszentmihalyi suggests, to help open up her thinking so she can produce the art to which she aspires.

Children are likely to be just as varied as adults in terms of their dispositions and their needs. So how do we ensure our learning environments nurture creativity in both teachers and children? Two examples of what teachers have considered and done within their spaces follow.

THE ALPHABET IN THE CLASSROOM

When young children begin to show signs of emerging literacy, it is common practice to have an alphabet along the wall as well as other supports for exploring print in the classroom. At the Halifax Grammar School, the four- and five-year-olds I worked with in the 2008/2009 school year were avid writers. They attempted to use print to communicate in meaningful ways, using both conventional and unconventional spelling, and were definitely comfortable taking risks with print.

In the fall semester, my coteacher and I decided to double the size of the writing area in response to children's engagement with print. I was loath, however, to introduce a commercially produced alphabet. Our teaching team worked hard to keep the classroom free of commercial posters and equipment, aiming to make the environment aesthetically pleasing through the use of natural materials, whimsical objects, light, fabric, and only children's work on the walls.

The children clearly needed an alphabet to refer to. One day I was alone in the classroom examining the children's work on the walls and thinking it needed updating. It occurred to me that if the environment was to be truly child-centered, the children themselves could create their own alphabet reference.

At small-group time, with about eight children who were keen writers, I explained the idea. It was met with huge enthusiasm. Rather than assigning letters to reproduce and illustrate, the children chose their favorite letters at first. They wrote the letters in upper and lower case on a piece of cardstock and chose some items to draw that would illustrate the letter. Some were unusual but meaningful to the child, such as the "XLR" one child chose for the letter *X*, referring to the car his mother drove. Over a matter of weeks, the whole alphabet evolved, with children working on this project both during small-group times and play.

▲ The alphabet, written and illustrated by children.

Of course, not all their letters were perfectly formed. Yet, the children understood that children's print is sometimes different from adults' and strived in other writing moments to form letters correctly using other supports. They knew exactly which children had drawn which illustrations and what stage of literacy that child was in. For example, a more accomplished child would comment "The *q* is not quite right, but she's still learning, so that's okay." or "When I'm five, I'll be able to write that better." This self-assessment proved to be a positive tool when, some months later, children were looking through their own portfolios where photocopies of their letters were placed.

PLACES FOR SOLITUDE

Being a part of a large group day in and day out can be hard work for young children. The noise level may be considerable, and the environment stimulating. If children are to have time to relax, daydream, think, or read, there must be places of solitude where they can retreat for a few quiet moments.

▲ A space for one also provides for sensory exploration. (Wee Care Developmental Centre in Halifax, NS)

▲ A child explores a quiet space created with a simple cardboard box and a curtain. (YMCA in Bridgewater, NS)

▲ These children created their own quiet space underneath a climbing frame, while other children played above them. Using available materials, they created a place to "relax in their house." (Children's School at Pacific Oaks College, CA)

Although space in many early childhood classrooms is in short supply, early childhood educators have found some wonderfully creative and inexpensive ways to provide solitude for children. Some unusual examples are shown on page 24.

Naomi's Journal

My latest challenge is the feeling that I need to clone myself! This week I've been responsible for the book area and studio. This was my first week in the studio, and also my first time experiencing art in an inquiry-based format. I know in many ways I am fighting against my natural tendencies to plan and control. I feel like slapping my own fingers for the near blasphemy to what the purpose of the art studio is. I need to remember that my job is to create a warm and inviting environment that encourages children to explore the materials and the many ways they can be used to represent their ideas and interests.

Multiple Languages for Representing Ideas

Our colleagues in Reggio Emilia, Italy, have done an outstanding job of provoking us to think deeply about our environments and the materials in them. These educators speak of the hundred languages children use to express their ideas and knowledge; that is, children have many symbolic ways in addition to using verbal or written language to show us their thinking. We may see children playing out their ideas through drama, music, physical activity, or art. Environments in Reggio Emilia include a central *piazza* or meeting place where the whole school can share ideas and an *atelier* (workshop or studio) where children can fully express their ideas using multiple types of media.

Inspired by the abundance of beautiful stuff and diverse media available to children in Reggio Emilia schools, other educators around the world have developed studio spaces or small niches that offer children more opportunities to express their ideas in multiple ways. Children who are not yet verbal or who prefer to articulate their ideas in graphic or sculptural ways then have an opportunity to express themselves. As an example, a child in my own classroom wanted to create an alien puppet and had a difficult time explaining how this would work. Given extensive time and an abundance of materials, he was able to make the puppet visible and to feel the satisfaction of his idea coming to life. Once the puppet was made, he was also able to verbally explain his ideas more clearly.

TAKING TIME

In my own classroom setting, I found four- and five-year-old children were often in a big hurry to complete projects and did not really understand the potential of materials in their studio corner. The teaching team's response to this was to try to slow down the process of exploring materials by having children continue to build on the previous day's work for several consecutive days. Children explored alternate types of surfaces to become aware of creating not only on paper but on cardstock, wood, three-dimensional surfaces, acetate, and so on. During a study of lines over several days, the children used numerous media to create designs.

This type of work provided both the children and me with time to think. We thought about foreground and background and examined these concepts in illustrations and art prints. We thought about layering and texture, what needed paint on top of it, and what needed paint around it. And we thought about what made things stick—not only glue! This type of deep exploration of materials was made possible not only by having the materials available in the environment but also by having the time to think about them and to talk about them with other children and teachers. This knowledge of materials empowered children to represent their ideas more fully in future projects.

▲ A multimedia piece, produced over several days. Beginning with card stock, children painted, drew, and applied yarn and tissue to their artwork.

Opening the Mind to Creative Thinking

While some people feel comfortable with the idea of thinking in ways that are new to them, others may find this causes some anxiety. Perhaps the latter have never had the freedom or opportunity to deeply examine their philosophy and how it is made visible in the work setting. Or perhaps they have not experienced the excitement of a precious moment when a truly new idea occurs to them and they are able to enact this idea in their classroom and then to watch how it plays out. All teachers deserve the opportunity to experience such moments and to have the freedom to collaborate with children and other teachers in order to explore new ideas and approaches. It is affirming to wonder "What if?" in response to children or to something you have read about and then to embark on a journey to find the answer to your question. To nurture your own creative thinking, here are some ideas for consideration.

Dare to imagine. When considering how to approach children's ideas, interests, and questions, let your mind encompass *all* the possibilities, even those that seem far-fetched or out of reach. Imagination feeds creativity. Before your left brain steps in to edit ("We couldn't possibly do that . . ."), imagine "What might happen if . . . ?" For every twenty or thirty ideas that enter your mind, one or two may be possible. But unless you have imagined in the first place what might be possible, there isn't a chance it will happen.

This approach is often used in corporate settings where creativity is valued, such as in the field of advertising. When a group comes together to brainstorm, *all* ideas are examined, even those seeming at first glance grandiose, strange, or impossible. Sometimes an idea that seems out of reach at first turns out to be possible after all.

Consider process versus product. We frequently use the phrase *process versus product* when referring to children's art or explorations. We value the child's process, since we understand that is how she makes sense of the world. The same holds true for adults. In order to nurture creative thinking, we need to think about our thinking (metacognition). Roger von Oech (2002, 35) in *Expect the Unexpected or You Won't Find It* explains, "When I'm relaxed and playful, there's a greater probability that unexpected things will flow my way." This relaxed mood and letting the mind drift and wonder is more conducive to creativity than staying focused on one narrow task or sticking with an old script. When thinking about your own thinking and processes, here are some questions to ask yourself:

- How often do I stop to rethink a previously held idea or approach?

- How do I prepare to approach things in a new way, to see something through a different lens? How do I get into the mood for imagining what might be?

- How do the children see a topic or activity? What about people from outside the field of teaching? What is the expert's take on your investigation of a topic?

- What am I curious about?

- What does my mind do when something unusual enters my consciousness? Do I dismiss it or embrace it? Do I jot down these thoughts and ideas?

- What kinds of processes do we have in place in our organization that support creativity and the development of new approaches?

Embrace complexity and ambiguity. Many teachers recognize the value of complexity in children's work, the connections children make between ideas and topics, and the many ways children are able to think about something and represent it. The work of teachers and children in Reggio Emilia reminds us of this complexity through their idea that children have a "hundred languages" to express what they know.

Along with complexity comes ambiguity. When children and adults explore something intriguing or unusual, the outcome or direction of the exploration is not always clear. This ambiguity can be troubling for some because it requires a willingness to wait and see what will evolve. Trusting in the process is essential even when feeling some disequilibrium. With careful documentation of the children's work, understandings, and misunderstandings and with notes about the teacher's thinking, the complexity of the children's learning and the paths you have taken together will become clearer.

Rather than embracing comfort, therefore, it is sometimes necessary to recognize disequilibrium as a sign of being on our "growing edge." This phrase, first introduced to me during my studies with Pacific Oaks College, aptly describes that place where we are stepping out of the familiar (what we already know and use) into the more unfamiliar "edge" where new growth occurs. This is an exciting place to be.

Examine everything. It is easy to slip into complacency when we work in the same setting or with the same teaching team year after year. If we reflect on our own work on a regular basis, during a weekly team meeting or a monthly staff meeting, we are more likely to think in depth about what we are doing. When examining our own work in relationship to children's thinking and ideas, there are questions we can ask ourselves:

- What puzzled the children through this exploration?

- What puzzled the teachers? How is this being addressed?

- How have we supported children's ideas?

- How does our environment support children's search for knowledge or their experimentation to find out? How is their thinking made visible?

- In what ways do we allow children to construct knowledge by following what seems to be a misunderstanding?

Lana's Story: Zi Hao and the Skeletons

In relation to the last question, here is an example from a teacher who allowed a child to find out about dinosaur skeletons. Lana O'Reilly works with the Toronto School Board as a junior kindergarten teacher and an art teacher for older grades. Below, she describes a situation in which a child for whom English is a second language was clearly puzzled about dinosaurs and their skeletons.

> Zi Hao was looking at a fiction book we had read called *What Pet to Get* by Emma Dodd. On one page was a cartoon-like picture of a dinosaur and on the next page was a picture of the dinosaur skeleton. The parent in the book was explaining that they could not have a dinosaur as a pet because dinosaurs are extinct. Zi Hao was flipping over and over the pages of the dinosaur and the skeleton.

ZI HAO: Where is the bone? The bone is come out here. Died? Is alive? This skeleton alive. That dinosaur died.

LANA: If it's just your bones can you be alive?

ZI HAO: Nooooo.

LANA: Because where is his brain and where is his heart?

ZI HAO: It's gone. It fall out. If you go like that, it's gone. You pull up this bone. Arm bone. This dinosaur has bones in here.

LANA: This is the . . .

ZI HAO: Skeleton.

LANA: Where is the skeleton?

ZI HAO: Inside. The skeleton inside.

LANA: Do you remember last year with the butterflies when you drew the

▲ Zi Hao examines an illustration of dinosaur bones.

baby butterflies and then you drew the cocoon over them? The skeleton is just like that—just like the baby butterfly inside the cocoon.

ZI HAO: The skeleton inside the dinosaur. The dinosaur extinct.

LANA: What does extinct mean?

ZI HAO: Died. Why he died? Where he go? Where skeleton now? I can draw bone here? The bone.

This conversation shows Lana was thinking hard about Zi Hao's thinking. She attempted to help him understand the concept of skeletons by using clarifying questions. The story continues.

Zi Hao was looking at another book. This one was nonfiction and had artist renderings of what dinosaurs may have looked like when they were alive.

ZI HAO: Look out bones. I see that part over there. That dinosaur is not dead. That dinosaur is dead. What happened to his skin?

LANA: It is so old that the skin rotted away. It is not there anymore—just the bones.

ZI HAO: Why would you open it out? The skeleton all come out? You open it out. What happened to his eyes? All of the skin and all of the eyes they pull out. What happen to the dinosaur? It just dead?

LANA: Dead. He died a long, long time ago.

ZI HAO: This real? He dead?

LANA: Are there dinosaurs today?

ZI HAO: Yes.

LANA: You told me before that they are extinct. What does extinct mean?

ZI HAO: It's died.

LANA: There are no more dinosaurs anywhere.

ZI HAO: Where the dinosaur go?

LANA: The dinosaurs are all gone. They are all dead. They are extinct.

ZI HAO: All the bones fall out? Why all the bones fall out?

LANA: I found this dinosaur book because I want to show you something.

ZI HAO: The skeleton. Why this dinosaur the skeleton? What happen to the bone? He take out the bone?

CHARLIE (another student walking by): The dinosaur dies and then the skin and everything else rots away and then just the bones are left.

ZI HAO: How they get bones?

CHARLIE: People find them. They put the bones back together.

ZI HAO: All of this come out (gesturing to the skin). And the bones come out.

LANA: What is that?

ZI HAO: Skeleton. No dinosaur skeleton. People. Why? They die?

LANA: That person is dead.

ZI HAO: They have no bones. The skeleton.

LANA: They have bones. Where are your bones?

ZI HAO: In there. Where the bone go? The skeleton. Inside you? You make the skeleton. You put that in there.

LANA: That's the skeleton inside you.

ZI HAO: Inside you? You make the skeleton go out in there. That the skeleton (gesturing to his stomach)?

LANA: That's your stomach.

ZI HAO: Have bone in there? In this? Bone?

LANA: Are there bones in there? No.

ZI HAO: Bones no there. Bones inside. Inside here (touching his arm).

LANA: Will you draw a skeleton for me?

Lana could sense Zi Hao's desire to understand as he began to relate skeletons to humans as well as to dinosaurs. And another child's expertise was brought into the puzzle. During the conversation, Lana had a wonderful idea she thought might help Zi Hao understand where the skeleton was.

Zi Hao drew a dinosaur on a piece of paper. Lana gave him a piece of acetate and asked him to draw the skeleton. He drew a skeleton of a dinosaur beside his dinosaur drawing. He looked at his drawings.

ZI HAO: No. That the dinosaur. It no hurt my dinosaur. Why he be extinct? All the bone is here. I can make that skeleton. All the bone has

▲ Zi Hao's dinosaur drawing.

been the skeleton. Why the bone outside? The dinosaur extinct. Put the bones outside.

LANA: That dinosaur is extinct? What is this part here?

ZI HAO: Eye hole. The eyes they fall out. But eyes can be in there.

LANA: Do skeletons have eyes in them?

ZI HAO: Nooo. (Goes back and looks in the dinosaur books.) That's different here. Why the dinosaurs extinct? I put all the bones in here. All the bones go on the floor. They fall right off. I put all the bones back he can come back again. Yes?

LANA: Who is coming back?

ZI HAO: The skeleton come back as a dinosaur. (Starts to draw bones on the acetate over his drawing of the dinosaur.)

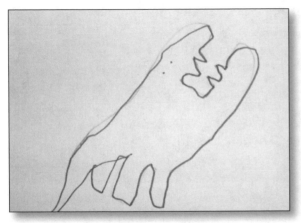

▲ Zi Hao uses an acetate overlay.

LANA: Do you think that can happen?

ZI HAO: Yes. I put three bones here. No bone there.

LANA: Why no bones there?

ZI HAO: Because extinct.

LANA: Zi Hao today you asked me why the dinosaurs are extinct. Why do you think they are extinct?

ZI HAO: The bones fall out.

LANA: How do the bones fall out of them?

ZI HAO: Because they extinct. They just did.

LANA: How did the bones fall out?

ZI HAO: They fall out like this (gesturing with his hand).

LANA: What do you think, Nate (another student)?

NATE: Well I think meteorites hit the earth and lots of dust from those spilled up into the air and blocked the sunlight so that the dinosaurs didn't have any sun left so they began to die out.

ZI HAO: These are the bones and then they fall out. Then this dinosaur he didn't have bones?

LANA: This is the same dinosaur. This is what he looked like when he was alive.

ZI HAO: The bones gone? Why? Where the bones?

NATE: For example, like all the dinosaurs died out from a meteorite hitting the earth from space.

LANA: I think Zi Hao is asking about this one dinosaur.

ZI HAO: Why is this one dinosaur get extinct? All the dinosaur not extinct.

LANA: What does extinct mean?

ZI HAO: No. This extinct.

NATE: That it's gone forever and it's never going to live again. But he might just make this one live again if he wants to (gesturing to Zi Hao's drawing).

LANA: Is this dinosaur extinct?

ZI HAO: No.

LANA: Why not?

ZI HAO: Because he has skin. This one he extinct.

LANA: Why?

ZI HAO: Because he have no skin. What happen? He fall down and the bone fall out. All the bone fall out of the dinosaur. That dinosaur extinct. All the skin fall out and now there no more dinosaur left. This dinosaur he extinct. All these dinosaur they extinct (gesturing to all the photos of the dinosaurs in the book). (Turns the page to find a human skeleton). People skeleton. Extinct.

LANA: Are people extinct?

ZI HAO: Yeah.

LANA: But we're here now. We're alive. Can we be extinct?

ZI HAO: No.

LANA: This one person is dead but are all the people dead?

ZI HAO: No. (Looks through the book and finds a horse skeleton.) This extinct.

LANA: Are all horses extinct? Are there horses that are alive today?

ZI HAO: Yes.

LANA: Is this dinosaur extinct?

ZI HAO: Yes. Bones. No skin.

LANA: Is this dinosaur extinct?

ZI HAO: No. Because skin here. The skin come back? We wait for the skin come back?

LANA: The skin can't come back because they are not alive anymore.

ZI HAO: The skin no come back. It's gone. (Turns the page to look at a snake skeleton that is an X-ray of a live snake.) The snake extinct? That one not alive.

LANA: That snake is alive. They took an X-ray, a special picture of his bones.

ZI HAO: The bones still inside. He not extinct.

LANA: What does extinct mean?

ZI HAO: Dead. But all the snake all the skin fall out then dies. All gone.

(Lana turns back to the dinosaur skeleton pictures.)

ZI HAO: Dinosaur. Dinosaur extinct.

LANA: Are there any more dinosaurs on Earth?

ZI HAO: No. The bones fall out. The skin not gonna come back. It stays out. No more. No more dinosaur.

Zi Hao and Lana were in a dance of collaboration. Other persons with more knowledge about the topic (the teacher and other students) tried to assist Zi Hao in understanding how there can be (that is, what appears to be) "real" dinosaurs in the book when they are extinct. The bones added to his puzzlement. So Lana used a creative approach with an unusual material—acetate—to explore what is inside versus what is outside. She hoped he would understand through many experiences and conversations what exactly *extinct* means and that the dinosaur skeletons were from extinct creatures. The conversations and Zi Hao's understanding took some time. Through careful listening, Lana was able to grasp what Zi Hao was thinking and respond to it.

Compare this thoughtful series of conversations to simply reading a book about dinosaurs to this child. Instead of expecting the child to learn through reading and listening, there was scaffolding going on. We can sense the teacher's thinking as much as the child's. Lana was listening carefully and taking the time to think about what to do next. Carlina Rinaldi refers to this practice as "a pedagogy of listening" (Wien 2008, 148). This approach is an important aspect of emergent curriculum. Children's articulated thoughts, along with their drawings and other representations, provide a window into their thinking.

Acting on Our Imagination

Perhaps in your own past you experienced a situation in which creativity seemed to be "taught out" of you in school. You are away from that situation now, and it is time to reclaim what was within you and all of us as children. Children, for the most part, are not self-conscious in their thinking. As in the earlier e-mail story, they are not afraid to put out there their theories about how they think the world works. This freedom to think out loud about how something might be, how it might work, or what they might do, empowers children to explore and imagine. Teachers deserve the same freedom.

In the previous chapter, which discussed the basic tenets of emergent curriculum, you read about reflection, dialogue, and flexibility. These same ideas exist when engaging in creative pursuits. Emergent curriculum and creative thinking are aligned; one feeds the other in a kind of dance. With an open mind, we can see what children are doing and hear what they are saying with no preconceived agendas. When we listen and watch and reflect before we act, we may find ourselves responding in original ways.

In the following chapters, you will read about educators of both children and adults who have seen familiar situations through a fresh lens. As their stories are presented, you will read how flexibility, reflection, dialogue, openness, responsiveness, and taking your time are all connected to a curriculum that is responsive and fresh and that allows you to think creatively about what you are seeing and hearing in the classroom.

3

Using Stories as a Means of Professional Development

Storytellers' priority is teacher growth. Storytellers have access to expertise—their own or borrowed—but they draw on it sparingly. Instead they look for the knowledge that teachers are already using and reflect it back to them, making teachers' own stories, rather than established authority, the starting point for learning.

—Elizabeth Jones

London Bridge Child Care Services in Ontario, Canada, is a large organization with fourteen early childhood centers that serve twelve hundred children from infancy to school age. With a staff of 350 educators, it makes sense that a full-time employee coordinates and develops professional development initiatives. Anne Marie Coughlin is the program director and professional-development coordinator for London Bridge. Over the years, she has recognized the importance of opportunities for teachers to tell their stories as a means of professional development.

Educators at London Bridge are inspired by the practices of Reggio Emilia and have been on the journey of examining and learning from these practices for over ten years. During this journey, they have visited places such as the St. Louis Reggio Collaborative schools in Missouri, the Boulder Journey School in Colorado, and the Chicago Commons schools. They have learned an enormous amount from listening to and reflecting on the stories shared by educators at these schools. And now they are ready to tell their own stories of professional exploration and development.

Stories from London Bridge

Anne Marie shares the story of London Bridge's staff development below. She believes that telling their own story—articulating to others what they do and why—will be a meaningful learning experience for everyone involved.

Early childhood educators have long understood the power that storytelling has in their classrooms. Along with the obvious benefits to children in terms of literacy and language development, we (the teachers and staff at London Bridge) have used stories to gather together with children, engage minds, inspire creativity, and make meaning of the world around us.

Although we understood the importance of using stories to support growth and development in children, we have overlooked the value of using stories to support our own growth as educators.

Part of the work we have been undertaking in our approach to professional development is to parallel what we offer educators with what we want educators to offer children. This work has led us to ask ourselves the following questions:

- What are the stories that resonate with us?

- How can we use stories to gather together as a learning community?

- How might we provide opportunities for educators to share their stories with each other?

- How can we use our stories to make meaning of what is happening in the classroom, to inspire each other, and as a tool to more effectively understand the development of both children and ourselves?

There are stories unfolding in our classrooms every moment of every day. While we know it is impossible to capture everything, it is valuable for us to recognize that significant things are continuously happening. By regularly giving attention to children's encounters and sharing them with each other, we begin to know these children more fully and find ourselves able to focus more on what they *can* do rather than what they can't. The following are some of the ways we have come to use our own stories to help answer some of these questions.

A Tale of Two Babies

Like many young babies, Skylar sat on the floor experimenting with the interesting sound he was able to produce when he moved his fingers across his lips and blew—that vibrating and delightful "raspberry" sound we adults are so familiar with. Sitting across from Skylar, watching with great interest, was Gavin. In a mimicking response, Gavin subtly brought his own fingers to his lips and moved them in the same fashion. But something was different. No noise came from his mouth. He paused for a moment and looked again at Skylar who was still joyfully producing sounds. He reached out and hit Skylar in the mouth, causing him to cry.

This is an important story for us as educators. By capturing this thirty-second interaction, we are able to interpret Gavin's actions and gain insight into his thinking and intentions:

- *I am interested in that noise you are making.* (I am curious.)
- *I will try it myself.* (I have a theory about how this works.)
- *It doesn't work the same when I try it.* (I make a discovery.)
- *Perhaps only your mouth can make that noise?* (I come up with a new theory and test it out.)

It could have been easy to miss that subtle exchange and make assumptions about what just happened.

What can we learn about children by giving their stories our time and consideration? How does how we see children affect the way we respond to them? Perhaps we might develop a mind-set of "What a brilliant little mind in action," as opposed to "We must teach him not to hit." We have learned that each interpretation can generate a different response by the educator. Through that response, we can either help guide a child's curiosity or cause great confusion.

By telling that story to others, it reminds us there are often things we miss. It forces us to reflect closely on our response to children in the classroom. We are reminded that behaviors are not random. Part of our role as educators is to focus on what the child is trying to do and form future responses from what we learn.

INTRODUCING CHARLIE

One of our centers was fortunate enough to receive, as a gift from a local veteran's hospital, a five-foot model of a raccoon named Charlie made out of chicken wire and bottle caps. Charlie's story started in 2007 when resident veterans, along with art instructors, created him to make a contribution to the community. Since the hospital is located in a large park setting, the veterans see raccoons regularly and often have stories to share about their encounters with them in the fields around the building. After two years of living in the hall outside the art studios at the hospital, Charlie was gifted to our center.

We knew that introducing something as big and unfamiliar as Charlie could be very frightening for young children and thus had to be carefully considered. Instead of simply bringing Charlie into a classroom full of toddlers, we devised a careful introduction. Our plan was to wheel Charlie down the sidewalk that runs along the toddler playground. This way, there would be a fence between the children and Charlie. We would ask the children's permission before bringing him into the playground. Those who might be slower to warm up to Charlie could use the space of the entire playground to keep their distance. The children's educators would provide them with encouragement and support. The center director would be in charge of Charlie, and a support staff would be brought in to capture this first encounter on video.

Charlie made his first appearance as planned, coming to the children while they were on the playground. From the moment she heard him moving down the sidewalk, Natalie was intensely engaged. When the children were asked if they would like Charlie to come into the playground, however, Natalie's apprehension was clear. She moved closer to her teacher and pointed a questioning finger back to Charlie, which we interpreted as her need to confirm that it was safe.

While several of the other children moved close to Charlie right away, Natalie remained cautious and sought security in the arms of her teacher, who supported her. Two-year-old Christian seemed to understand Natalie's apprehension. When she was back on her own feet, Christian reached out in encouragement and support in a gentle and loving way. Without words, he took her hand and walked her over to Charlie. Christian touched him, offering a careful demonstration of how the bottle caps rattled. He encouraged Natalie to touch Charlie by touching the raccoon again and then moving aside for her to come closer. When he noticed Natalie's hat was covering her eyes, he attentively bent down and tried to lift it out of the way. Christian showed great patience; while he seemed intent on getting Natalie to touch Charlie, he allowed her the time she needed to warm up to him. Over time, Christian convinced Natalie to touch Charlie, and they went on to explore him together.

This story reminds us of the strong sensitivity and awareness young children possess. Christian's insightful approach demonstrated his understanding of both Natalie's reluctance and her desire to get closer to Charlie. At only two years old, he gently guided Natalie through a process we might consider reserved for the adult. And, like many toddlers, Christian is a biter!

How does this story influence how we see Christian (and others like him)? It moves us beyond the idea that he is "the biter" and helps us to see him instead as someone who is incredibly in tune with and empathetic toward someone else. He understands, even though no words have been exchanged. He is gentle and persuasive. He doesn't give up on Natalie and tries different strategies to engage and support her.

Christian reminds us of our obligation to look deeper, to pay close attention, and to not jump to conclusions. How different might this encounter have been if Christian's helpful gestures had been viewed as acts of aggression? How often has such an interpretation been made in the past? What else have we missed and at what cost? Reflecting helps us to understand this is not simply a story about a giant raccoon but also one about the competencies of children and our willingness to see them.

Such stories are examples of the importance of looking closely. They remind us of how easy it is to misread a child's intention and how quickly our well-intentioned actions can cause more harm than good.

It is through these seemingly ordinary moments that we discover the extraordinary.

▲ A supporting teacher.

▲ A reassuring hand.

▲ A careful demonstration.

▲ A helpful gesture to see better.

▲ A shared curiosity.

▲ A newfound confidence.

We post these stories for families to read and to serve as written records of what children can do. We share them with each other and use them as a reflection tool in our own practices. These stories fuel our conversations each day and deepen our relationships with both children and their families. Some of the ways in which we share our stories follow.

Make the most of staff meetings. Instead of giving attention to a laundry list of issues or tasks, we try to use this valuable time to share stories that unfold in our classrooms. This is a time when we can give voice to both the children's stories and to our stories as educators. The benefits of sharing stories in our staff meetings include

- building stronger relationships among educators as they build trust in each other by sharing their work;

- keeping children in the forefront of conversations;

- maintaining a sense of community within the center as educators gain a greater understanding of what is happening in each other's rooms;

- sharing resources or shared explorations;
- nurturing energy and excitement so educators leave the meetings in a positive manner rather than feeling resentment about giving up their time.

Set aside time in workshops and trainings. While lectures may be effective in some circles, we often find the most valuable learning happens when educators have opportunities to listen to each other, share viewpoints, and construct meaning together. This is why we feel it is important for workshops to provide educators with many opportunities to use their own stories as catalysts for reflection. Whereas workshops and trainings have specific topics, we use a facilitator-led approach to support and guide educators to share their own stories in order to make the topic more meaningful and relevant in their own lives.

Organize an annual project-sharing night. Throughout the year, many educators work on projects or investigations with the children that can sometimes last up to ten months. Once a year, we provide an opportunity for these educators to share their work with each other.

Make stories visible to children and families. We display our stories on the walls of the classroom, in children's portfolios, in the hallways and common areas, and in newsletters.

Use children's storybooks. Children's stories can often be intriguing and valuable in adult learning. They can be used to gather people together and set a tone for an evening, to give emphasis to a particular topic, to bring attention to important messages, or to simply inspire us.

Adults Sharing Their Work

Anne Marie's examples of story sharing illustrate that teachers need time to talk with each other. This is especially true in programs that are exploring sophisticated approaches or are engaged in a learning journey. When teachers share stories, it is clear that they are able to think about events from many perspectives and perhaps gain new understanding of what has happened.

When London Bridge embarked on a study of this new approach to teaching and learning with children, they began very gently by talking and embracing ideas as people became more comfortable. Over time, they have created their own version of Reggio-inspired approaches, a new philosophy statement, and new and creative ways of approaching professional development. Rather than trying to "wow the audience" through their presentations to each other, they are honest and frank, able to share their struggles as well as their successes. They continue to explore, taking time for reflective practice and using their core beliefs to develop their programs.

These shared stories of professional development show that learning for adults can be just as active, meaningful, creative, and inspired as we try to make learning for young children. Vygotsky taught us that for children learning is socially constructed. Why wouldn't this be the case for adults as well?

Educational settings, whether for early childhood or the later grades, can benefit when teachers tell their stories and share their work. Some simple, time- and cost-effective ways to encourage reflective dialogue and learning follow.

Create a classroom log. This can be as simple as having an open notebook or binder on top of a surface that is easily accessible to teachers. Into this log, teachers jot notes about what is occurring in the classroom, questions that arise from teachers as well as children, struggles and successes the teachers experience. This running record provides a shared place for teachers to "hold in mind" the myriad of interesting and challenging events that happen during a day, and it is a wonderful discussion-starter when teachers get together for dialogue.

Organize lunchtime learning opportunities. Whenever possible, the teachers at the elementary school where I work come together on Fridays to learn from each other. Having recognized that within our own organization we have a wealth of experiences and knowledge, we believe it is important to share our expertise. This is not only uplifting and validating, it is also a valuable venue for discussion and learning. It costs nothing except our time and open minds. Topics are suggested by the teachers who either want to learn about a particular topic or want to share their own enthusiasm or expertise with others. Some suggestions for future discussions have included writing poetry with children, watercolor painting, music in learning, and assessment.

Share documentation. Whether our documentation consists of a series of photographs, a book with photos and text, or panels that tell the story of a learning experience, it provides a chance for us to share. In some settings, documentation is considered a way to share learning journeys with parents and to revisit the journey with children. Documentation certainly achieves this. It can also be a tool to prompt reflection and dialogue between teachers, providing a chance for other educators to ask questions and to think about their own inquiries with children.

Whether you choose to tell your teaching story through words or through photographs, our whole profession benefits when we share. Perhaps conference organizers in the future will consider opportunities for sharing our stories as part of the agenda. Time for dialogue with each other is just as important as listening to presentations. When we listen to each other and when we try to articulate our own thinking, we are stepping into an active role in our own learning. As Parker Palmer (1998, 147) explains, "As we listen to each other's stories, we are often reflecting silently on our own identity and integrity as teachers."

Telling our stories, throughout the day or during meetings or at conferences, is far from being a waste of time or a luxury. It is a necessity because we learn from each other. We become more creative and reflective when we listen to others and compare their approaches with our own—stretching our thinking and challenging long-held ideas and scripts. We grow when we are listening actively to stories of real classroom life, offering our own opinions, and articulating what we believe.

The next chapter includes an example of real classroom life. Melissa starts a project with an idea from the children and is led to reflect on her own classroom environment in the process.

4

Taking Time to Make Lemonade

In any formative relationship, time is the necessary element for creating the relationship. So a school that forms is a school that gives time—time to children, time to teachers, time for their being together.

—Carlina Rinaldi

What happens when children are given unlimited time to explore a topic that naturally engages them? When teachers take extended time to observe carefully and respond thoughtfully, deep and meaningful learning can occur for both children and teachers.

Melissa is a seasoned teacher with twenty-five years of experience in early childhood education, nine of which have been at the Children's School at Pacific Oaks College in Pasadena, California. She works with two other teachers and a group of twenty-four four-year-olds in a half-day program. The team meets after class each day to reflect on the morning and to think about next steps for curriculum.

Since the Children's School is a demonstration setting for the college, the teachers and administration strive to use best practices in early childhood education based on developmentally appropriate practices and emergent curriculum. The teaching team observes closely and responds to those observations after reflection and discussion.

The Children's School, set in a pleasant California climate, is able to offer children outdoor play opportunities throughout the day. The outdoor setting is large and full of oak trees, with a natural garden, sandbox, spacious deck, climbing structure, and big porch on the front of the classroom.

Stories from the Children's School at Pacific Oaks College

Following a summer when many children attended summer school at the Children's School, Melissa and her colleagues watched with interest as the children played out their "big idea" of a lemonade sale over a lengthy period of time. Here, in Melissa's words, is what happened first.

> A small group of four-year-olds, only four children to begin with, began playing "lemonade sale" out in the yard using sand, water, and leaves for the lemonade, with plastic cups for serving. The provocation for this particular group began with prior knowledge from observing older children conducting a sale out in our community space, Shady Lane, the previous summer. More and more of the four-year-olds joined in this play and carefully prepared the lemonade, creating recipes by conversing back and forth about the right ratios. Then they went around the yard and asked teachers and children if they would like to buy a glass. Instead of using paper for money, they used leaves to represent currency. If a glass of their lemonade was five dollars, for example, the children would count out five leaves, hand it to the other children, and have the recipients pay them with the "money." This activity went on for about a month with daily changes taking place in how they would conduct the sale, where they would place the table for the sale, and how they would go about creating changes in the recipe. As time

passed, almost the whole group of twenty-four children joined this project.

Several weeks passed as the children continued with variations of selling and preparing lemonade and other items for sale. During the fourth week, the children initiated making signs for their sale. They got their own paper and pens, sat at a table with friends, and asked a teacher for correct spelling. A whole morning was dedicated to this activity. Then the signs went up and the pretend sale began.

▲ A child makes a sign for the lemonade sale.

Melissa's description shows the leisurely pace at which this project unfolded. There was no instant response from the teachers except to watch and listen closely. The play idea developed over the course of a month, and we can see children's deep engagement as they negotiated the recipe, how the sale would be set up, and what was needed to market their product. There was, no doubt, much measuring, mixing, counting, and writing going on. Along with this explicit academic learning, it is clear these teachers also had respect for the play and for how much time it takes a big play idea to fully develop. The teachers allowed the children to pursue their own path, to be in charge of their play, and to take their time figuring out what should happen next.

"What happens next" is a point many practitioners struggle with. We do not want to interfere with children's ideas; yet, at the same time, we want to scaffold further learning and engagement from what the children are presently doing. There is a fine balance here, and taking time to think helps prevent us from stepping over the line that divides child-initiated learning from teacher-led agendas.

Since the children were already selling lemonade in their play, Melissa and her colleagues took this into consideration and decided to offer the chance to sell real lemonade in the school community. Melissa continues her story.

The teaching team and the children decided to prepare for a real lemonade sale. As a group, we asked the families for donated lemons from local trees after discovering lemons were expensive to buy at the store. Children squeezed the lemons using old glass juicers. The juicing went on for days. One of our teachers tried

A child juices a lemon.

different recipes with the children, as we discovered that different varieties of lemons combined with sugar have different flavors.

Next we began working on our signs. This involved using poster paint and large pieces of paper. The project was a collaboration of ideas. With support from teachers, several children wrote on a single board. The children patiently waited their turn to add a word or an idea.

More signs were created over the next week. These signs were individual drawings from the children. Then the signs were distributed around the school, and the whole school community was invited.

Our sale was ready to begin. We set up shop in Shady Lane and had to negotiate how many people would be needed for each shift. In our meeting time, it was decided that groups of five children would take turns pouring the lemonade, handing the lemonade to the customer, taking the money from the customer, and giving it to the banker. The children waiting for a turn patiently sat on the rocks behind the sale and observed.

In this story, the collaborative nature of emergent curriculum is described. Working together, with teachers supporting children's efforts, both children's and teachers' voices are included in the ensuing activities. Again, the pace is leisurely—there is no rush. There were days and days of juicing, recipe testing, and making signs. It might have been easier for a teacher to provide a recipe for the children and tell them which juicer would work best, but a tremendous learning opportunity would have been missed. Instead, the children and teachers had to use trial and error and come to consensus—no easy feat when several four-year-olds are involved, yet it was such an important part of learning to participate in group work. When children are involved in decision making, they are more likely to show patience and determination; this is, after all, *their* work and it becomes worthwhile for the children to persist.

What happens once real money becomes involved? In our society, the natural course of events is, of course, to spend it! The children had another decision to make, and Melissa describes what happened.

▲ A child paints a sign for the lemonade sale.

> After every sale, during our community meeting, we would count the money aloud to record the profits. Then the question we had for the group was, "What are we going to do with the money?"
>
> After brainstorming with the children, we unanimously voted to donate the money to a local animal shelter. Animals had been another ongoing central theme with the children. We contacted the shelter and tried to arrange for a field trip. But time for an actual field trip had run out, so instead we scheduled a representative from the shelter to come out to collect the money.

This project continued to be meaningful to the children as they made a decision about how to spend the money. Note that this decision was made *after* the money was raised. These teachers realized the process of the sale and the play around it was most important for the children. They did not raise the idea of money beforehand—as in "let's raise money for . . ."—but waited instead until the sale was complete and money had been collected. Then there was a reason to think about money, and the children and staff connected their ongoing interest in animals to help them make this decision.

As with all long-term projects, things did not come to a shuddering halt once the sale was over. Rather, the teachers noticed other tangents occurring naturally and took care to follow up on these.

> Many extensions developed out of this project beyond the sale in Shady Lane. Other groups were invited over for a free cup of lemonade. We also visited a small local grocery store and had a behind-the-scenes tour to develop a deeper understanding of a business. We juiced other fruits and discovered the labor involved in hand juicers. We tried different types of juicers, yet the glass juicers were a favorite.

These ideas were all generated from the children. We supported their interests and created extensions by supplying materials, suggesting different ideas from our own prior experiences, and gathering ideas from the children's experiences. We also involved both the school and the greater community in our project. The project began in October and went on throughout the year.

The fact that this project lasted until June is a testament to how it engaged the children. It's easy to imagine they will always remember the school year they created a business out of their own ideas, and that they developed and ran it themselves.

Naomi's Journal

I have been having difficulty coordinating the activities in the studio and the book center and then listening, observing, and writing down the things I hear and see. I had to stop myself yesterday when half of the morning had gone by and I realized I hadn't really seen or heard anything, let alone written down those observations. What needs to change?

There's a part of me that's been feeling that I'm not doing my job if I'm not planning new activities/experiences for the children every day. This weekend I stopped to examine that feeling and realized where it may be coming from. When teaching under a standardized curriculum (and I use the word under literally, since sometimes it can feel like a heavy hand pressing down on teachers), there is such a tremendous pressure to go, go, go in order to meet all the outcomes. Rarely is the value of slowing down and/or revisiting recognized.

This is one instance where I realize I cannot trust my feelings. One of the parts of emergent curriculum that I remember reading about is the concept of freeing ourselves from the reign of time. I need to pay less attention to my calendar and clock and tune in to the children and let my readings of them and their learning set the pace for my planning.

Teachers' Reflections Lead to Use of Natural Materials

The children weren't the only ones learning during this time. The teachers, who watched children's engagement with natural materials at the beginning of this project, also reflected on the natural environment in general and how it affected the children.

When teachers keep their minds open and alert, there is always a window of opportunity for taking a new look at their own practice. Here, in Melissa's words, is an interesting reflection on how the children's actions caused the teachers to rethink some of their decisions about the physical environment.

Our group of children always seemed to gravitate toward raw materials and would increasingly add them to existing activities. For example, rocks and sticks displayed in other parts of the classroom would be added to playdough to make different foods and animal habitats. Leaves were collected outside and brought inside to be used in the housekeeping area. Large tree branches lying around the yard would turn into horses, swords (a challenge for teachers), and other objects of power. Children had serious inquiries about nature and animals, which we supported through books, pictures, and animal figures.

After this observation, we decided to think more deeply about what type of materials we were using with the children. We brought an Andy Goldsworthy book into the classroom and displayed pictures of his natural art. Pinecones, polished rocks, and other materials were used as inspired by Goldsworthy's work. Children who never previously visited the writing and art tables created their own interpretations of art figures from the book. Some children used sticks to create letters and even attempted to make self-portraits. Our teaching team continued to think of ways to provide different media for art, blocks, and sensory material so children might express themselves and build a greater understanding of nature in general.

One day we decided to visit a natural setting directly across the street called the Arroyo. Instead of just hiking in the Arroyo, which we had done in the past with children, we selected an area near a large climbing hill and let the children play. We took along other materials, such as crayons, playdough, and a few other things, in case the children ran out of things to do, but those materials were never touched. The children ended up playing for three hours on the hill, climbing to the top, building pretend campfires using leaves and sticks, sliding down the dirt hill, searching for treasure, and sitting on a large tree stump that overlooks the mountain.

After leaving the Arroyo, we realized the children had played for three hours without one single toy. The old tree stump turned into an airplane or rocket ship that propelled children into the sky. The dirt hill provided a physical challenge, as they attempted to find ways of climbing without slipping down. When at the top, they slid down using the smooth dirt path as a slide. The eucalyptus leaves and pods were their treasures, as were interesting-looking rocks. We encountered many different types of insects, some we couldn't identify. When we returned to school, we brought out an insect resource and figured out that one innocent looking centipede was actually very poisonous.

After several Arroyo experiences, we began to look at our classroom materials differently. We reevaluated everything in the space down to the colors we added to the water in the sensory table, colors in the playdough, and colored paper. Why were we using hot pink and bright yellow? How could we bring in colors from our environment that fit the context of our school? We decided to stop adding food coloring to the water and playdough and limited the use of artificial color to only our paints (many of our materials are store purchased and are—no surprise—bright colors). As a result, the playdough use extended to other things in addition to food. Through our observations, we noticed the water table work also seemed more calming to the children.

As we continued to rethink the environment, we began to see the value of representation using organic materials. The ideas these materials provoked from the children were thoughtful and complex. For example, children who would typically never visit the art table found their own language using sticks and rocks to represent their ideas. They began to see themselves as artists and inventors. An increased interest in insects, plant life, and minerals was genuine, and more threads were created from these investigations.

Other threads that evolved from the children's experiences included animal habitats, which were constructed from objects found in the yard; wire work, using beads attached to large tree branches found in nature; documenting changes in the physical environment in the Arroyo due to our mild change in seasons; and a tangible understanding of water conservation.

Examining Old Practices

When teachers take the time to reflect, using their observations of children's play, conversations, and use of materials as a starting point, they create an opportunity to rethink their own practices. This is always a worthwhile endeavor, no matter how wonderful we think our learning environments are. Looking through another's lens and seeing the work or environment from their perspective leads to reflection about *why* we do what we do in every aspect of our practice.

In this case, the teachers reexamined their usual practice of providing materials and equipment in bright colors, ready-made and purchased from early childhood equipment suppliers. The children's fascination with organic materials led them to make changes.

When we engage in observation, reflection, and response, we can think of ourselves as social scientists. We collect data from our work with children, engage in dialogue with peers to interpret what it may mean, form an educated guess about "what would happen if," and create a new environment to test our hypothesis. Whatever happens, we are providing an opportunity for the environment or curriculum to become richer and more intriguing. In the case of this classroom, a richer curriculum did not mean "more complex" or "more stuff" but, rather, a simplification of what was already there and changes that actually built on the children's use of natural materials.

This kind of thinking on the part of teachers requires a disposition of openness to new approaches and a willingness to try new things. Although, for some individuals this may result in a feeling of disequilibrium, this kind of creative thinking and response can develop into a habit of thought to fuel our passion for our teaching practice.

If we remain open and watch carefully, children's projects can lead to reflection about our own taken-for-granted practices and environments. Sometimes this will lead to a change for the better and, at the very least, to making careful considerations about everything we do in our teaching practice.

In the next chapter, one story is from a teaching team who engaged in careful considerations about one child that led to a project for everyone. Another story is from a teacher who had to consider the children's agenda when it veered in an unexpected direction. In both cases, teachers reflected and responded, and a new direction emerged.

5

Embracing the Unexpected: Explosions (and Penguins!)

Observing children's interests requires a conscious mental set of flexibility, like leaving a space, or creating an opening in the teacher's agenda, in which something unexpected might appear.

—Carol Anne Wien

Susan Hagner and her colleagues at Emerson School for Preschoolers in Concord, New Hampshire, have long engaged in emergent curriculum, taking time to think about the underlying meanings of children's play and responding to children's thinking with care, creativity, and deep thought. So when one boy who loved to draw began to focus on wars, planes, bombs, and space wars, the team approached this somewhat disruptive play with their usual thoughtfulness. They asked themselves, "How can we channel this intense interest?" "What is this really about?" and "What are his needs?"

It is not unusual and is in fact becoming more and more common to see children acting out aggressive or violent scenarios during their play in early childhood settings. Inevitably, this causes consternation for the educators. Most teachers strive to facilitate children's learning about conflict resolution, peaceful and respectful problem solving, and the development of social skills within a group. When we see children in play shooting each other or showing an intense interest in war, it sets off alarm bells for us. Some teachers tend to simply forbid this type of play, but we have all seen children who create guns from just about anything in their environment. Other teaching teams try to work *with* the play and get to the root of this interest.

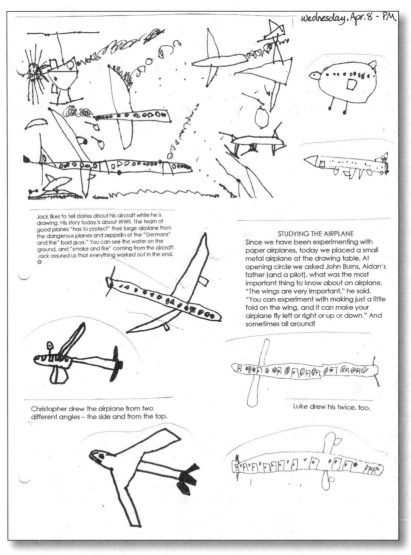

▲ Children's drawings of planes and explosions.

Susan's Story: Thinking about Explosions

The Emerson team decided to watch carefully and see what the play consisted of. They saw an active child engaged in lots of movement who often acted out explosions. As the team thought further about explosions, they wondered if an investigation of them would interest the child as well as other children. They provided a provocation, asking the group, "What causes explosions?"

At the same time on the other side of the world, a real volcano was about to erupt. With support from adults, the children easily tracked this news online. Recognizing an opportunity, the staff provided some invitations for children. Every day there was an experiment for the children to try involving various ways to erupt, explode, fizz, or rumble things. As in any true scientific exploration, the children were asked to predict what would happen, draw their thoughts, observe, and plot the course of the explosion.

Some samples follow of the rich documentation from these early days when every possible type of explosion was explored, from bubble popping to volcanoes, paint splatters, and bread dough imploding.

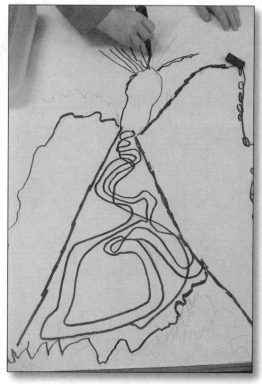

▲ Representations of explosions using a variety of media.

DOCUMENTATION COMMUNICATES THE STORY

The role of pedagogical documentation in this project was important. Since the children at Emerson were in two part-time groups, the work in each group often took different paths. In this case, the original child was in one group, while in the other group there was a great deal of parent input.

The murals take form over time, with input from all of the children. They are an impressive representation of the children's thinking.

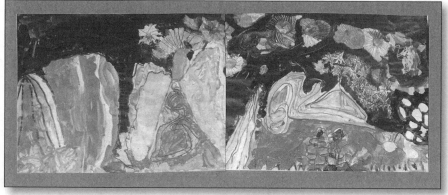

▲ The finished murals.

Documentation became an important communication tool between the two groups. As in life, enthusiasm within the classroom is contagious. Children in one group were very interested in the thoughts, opinions, and theories of the other group.

Plentiful documentation explains the children's journey in learning about explosions and volcanoes.

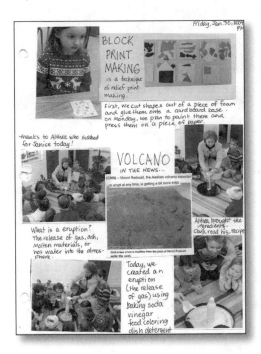

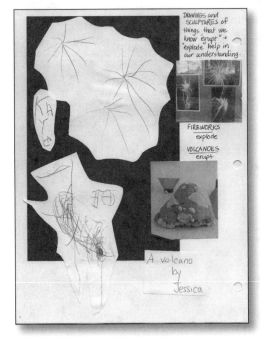

Emergent curriculum sometimes comes out of challenging situations that prompt open-minded thinking about why children are doing or thinking certain things or acting in a particular way. When we are alert to possibilities and can imagine approaches that work *with* children instead of trying to change them, wonderful trajectories can emerge.

Teachers must be open to the unexpected ideas that come from children even when we think we know where the curriculum is heading.

Michelle's Story: Something Unexpected

At Giant Steps Children's Centre in Tantallon, Nova Scotia, the preschool teachers spent several weeks in the fall supporting the children's interest in winter animals. Michelle Tessier, one of the teachers, describes what happened.

> It was getting colder at the end of October/early November, and we were talking about that. The children were talking about which animal could tolerate the cold. Conversations moved quickly to the North Pole and the animals that live there. So my teaching partner, Angelique, and I thought we would go to the library and get some books on penguins and other animals. We brought the books in a few days later and displayed them in our own classroom library. When story time came, I asked the children if they would like to read a book about penguins, thinking if they showed interest we would delve further into this topic with them. The group, predominately boys, yelled, "Yeah, the penguins!" and "Yeah, the Pittsburgh Penguins!"
>
> Astonished, I replied, "I mean the penguins that live in the Arctic . . . " and held up the penguin book complete with real photos. But, again, "Yeah! The Pittsburgh Penguins!" By this time, more and more children were joining in the cheer and chattering excitedly to each other about hockey, the Penguins, hockey gear, who had a real stick, or whose brother played.
>
> I sat there with my penguin book and looked over at Angelique. We spent that entire winter playing hockey, researching hockey, wearing jerseys, bringing in sticks, quoting rules, building a Zamboni, and learning the national anthem.

Although completely taken aback at first, the teachers quickly regrouped and responded. Knowing the children well, they fully understood how penguins in

▲ The best hockey hug.

▼ The "Zamboni" takes to the "ice."

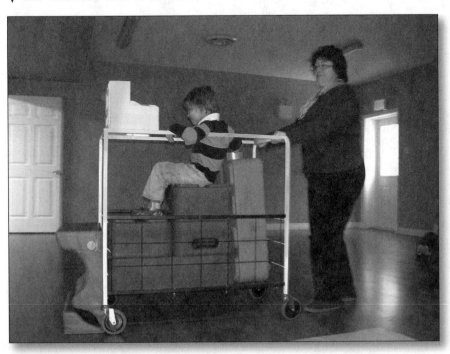

the children's minds would refer to the hockey team. Their families, fathers in particular, were consumed with hockey, and many played competitively at the local level. Therefore, these children had prior knowledge about how things worked at the arena, what the rituals were, and how to play.

This project quickly developed into a creative collaboration. The children were adamant about what has to happen at a hockey game, and many times they took the lead in deciding how to use the gym as a hockey arena. For example, they informed their teachers that all the players must be announced by name in a loud, deep voice before they skated onto the ice. Their number also had to be announced. Michelle dutifully took on the role of announcer.

Then the national anthem had to be sung. The two or three girls in the class who only occasionally pretended to play hockey and were not particularly interested in this project nevertheless were happy to oblige before continuing with their own play and projects.

The teaching team provided a way for the children to construct a much-needed piece of equipment—a Zamboni—by commandeering an old trolley. The children added a cardboard carton and a cushion, and the ice-cleaning machine was ready for action.

THE PROJECT DEVELOPS NEW TANGENTS

What kinds of underlying meanings were discovered by reflecting on this play? Michelle noted the children understood the idea of teamwork. When playing in the gym, for example, they would declare "we won" (referring to the Stanley Cup) and hug each other. They would also pretend to fight on the ice, which is, after all, a regular aspect of hockey games. They also understood the idea of the referee, what "gentleman's hockey" is, and that the whistle is a necessary part of the game.

Although the children were totally consumed for several months by this focus on hockey, the teachers noticed that when the children's focus began to change, other interests emerged that included issues of power, strength, and masculinity. When the children were outside, for example, they would play at camping by using rocks to make fire pits. This is not unusual in itself. But when Michelle introduced the phrase "stewards of the earth" during conversations about caring for the forest, the boys began to play at guarding the perimeter by surrounding their play space. With serious facial expressions, they would stand at attention and use deep voices for up to ten minutes at a time.

The teachers watched with interest as these investigations of power and strength unfolded. The children's play provided the teachers with opportunities to remind children that when they grew bigger and stronger they should look out for people who are smaller than them. In response to this, the children became protective of toddlers on the playground, speaking to them in deep and "adult" voices.

This outdoor play changed once again as the celebration of Sir Edmund Hillary's conquest of Mount Everest drew near. The anniversary was in the news, and Michelle brought this to the children's attention. The children began to play at climbing Mount Everest on a small hill in the backyard. They used ropes, ladders, and oxygen tanks made out of plastic bottles. Over and over again, they played out the drama of crossing over a crevasse, designing different types of ladders, climbing over chairs, and rappelling backward down the small slope. Then the teachers would throw the ropes down, and the children would climb back up. There was dramatic falling, struggling, and rescue, which again involved strength, daring, and courage.

Reflecting on Children's Agendas of Power and Strength

When we observe play that is rambunctious or full of rough and tumble action, and when we observe play that involves yelling, pushing, and chasing, we sometimes worry. One of our tasks as teachers is to keep children safe, and our classrooms should be somewhat calm and orderly. Yet we know children need this type of play. They need to act out danger, daring, and risk to see what it feels like, to learn how to be safe, to understand how to work with others in these situations, and to know what to do when other groups are "against" them. This is part of daily life in group settings and sometimes in life itself, and we can help children by paying attention to it rather than immediately putting an end to it.

Young children in today's society experience several kinds of stress, from the birth of a new sibling or moving into a new home to a parent being away at war or losing a job. Play is the medium in which children work through their emotions and deal with stress. Play often needs to be physically active, with opportunities for many kinds of interactions (including loud ones), and it needs to be child-initiated. Conversely, sometimes children need to be alone in a quiet place in order to de-stress. Children may need both outlets available at different times of the day or for different stresses.

How might we support children in releasing stress? Children should have

✓ ample time and space to play out scenarios over and over again, if necessary;

✓ teachers who observe and listen carefully, offering an empathetic ear when needed;

✓ a place to be noisy and rambunctious both indoors and outside;

✓ an opportunity to further represent their play through drawing, drama, music, or dictating stories to teachers who will act as scribes;

✓ boundaries, both physical and in terms of routines and expectations, that are reasonable and consistent while allowing for flexibility in response to individual children's needs.

The teaching teams in the previous examples paid attention to what children were doing and kept an open mind, considering such factors as the underlying meaning of the children's actions, how they could explore with the children, and how all the children could benefit from these investigations.

As a result of teachers' flexibility and reflection, positive outcomes occurred. Children could explore strong feelings of power and excitement while building on their prior knowledge. The result was much more rewarding and beneficial than it would have been if the teachers had forbidden the children's explosive and aggressive play. In their safe and caring environments, these children were able to experiment and learn while being loud, strong, and vigorous. They will surely remember their study of explosions and the Penguins into their adulthood, and perhaps they will share these delightful and unusual experiences with their own children.

In the next chapter, the story of another group of children who explored volcanoes is shared. Their story includes highly physical play that resulted in deeper relationships and understanding among all the players.

6

The Flexibility of Routines, Responses, and Teacher Roles

There's a way to do it better—find it.

—Thomas Edison

When examining old scripts, one of the first places to begin is by taking an honest and thoughtful look at routines. As educators, and together with the children in our classrooms and programs, we are embedded in routines. While it is true that young children thrive on the predictability and reassurance of their familiar routines, this doesn't mean we cannot create flexible and adaptable routines or events in response to children's needs and ideas. In order to reflect on routines, it is important to think about such things as the following:

- Why does this particular part of the routine occur at this time of day?

- How do the children respond to this?

- How rigidly do we adhere to time frames?

- If everything is organized by the clock, why is this?

- Who imposes these requirements, and why?

- How else could we organize time frames, if not by the clock?

- What leads us to change activities when we do?

It may be difficult to think creatively about this issue since much of the world is organized in a seemingly logical, time-driven way and since many of us are dependent on the clock when thinking about what happens in our workplace.

Naomi's Journal

I've felt like a fish out of water for these last few weeks. When considering trying out an inquiry–based approach, it is recommended that teachers find a comfortable entry point. There has been nothing comfortable about jumping into someone else's classroom with both feet and having to plan and follow an approach that I've only read about in books. Add to that the tendency I have to expect perfection of myself, the long hours I've been spinning my wheels trying to plan . . . I think I really do deserve that chocolate!

Introducing Stepping Stones

Stepping Stones Children's Center in Burlington, Vermont, is a full-time, privately operated multiage facility serving thirty-five families with children ages two to five years at a ratio of twenty children and four teachers per day. The teaching staff has a flexible approach to routines; their decisions about what will happen next are driven by the children's actions and curiosity. Their current open-style schedule is intentionally designed to enable as much free time as possible for children and teachers to engage in emergent work. Within basic times frames (for arrival, play, meals, and so on), there is much flexibility around how the staff members work, what they work on, and which children they work with, as well as how much time is spent on projects or extraordinary moments of learning. Teachers are also given a great deal of freedom about how they use their own strengths, interests, and abilities to collaborate with the children.

Liz's Stories: The Transition Teacher and Volcanoes

Liz Rogers has taught at Stepping Stones for over eighteen years and very much appreciates the culture of creativity that exists at the school. Some things that happen at the school, she explains, are responses to real-life joys or events, and emergence comes from responding—*layering onto* events through relationships—and from listening and paying attention. Liz continues in her own words.

Nurturing a culture of creativity requires not only paying attention to the interests, curiosity, and projects that grow between children and their teachers but also paying attention to the ways we structure our days to enable the possibility of inventive thinking and creative adventures to emerge and catch fire.

When we decided as a staff that we wanted to take an emergent approach to our learning with children, we also found that we had to actively explore ways to transform from our traditionally prescriptive style schedule (one directed by clocked transitions) to our current open format. During this shift, we invented the role of the transition teacher, who essentially acts as a steward or guide of our daily program routines. We have organized ourselves so that full-time teachers work four ten-hour days a week (7:30 a.m.– 5:30 p.m.), and each teacher has a set day when they are the transition teacher (also lovingly known by the children as the kitchen teacher). Knowing who the kitchen teacher is and who is teaching on the floor that day affects how we in the learning community anticipate and organize our daily course of action, in the same way that we would anticipate spending a day with a particular friend. We don't so much rely on the clock to tell us what to do but rather are motivated by the connections and opportunities that arise.

The transition teacher's focus is on greeting the families as they arrive, answering the phone, keeping track of special circumstances and medications, organizing snacks and lunch, and assisting children with self-care activities. It is a physically demanding job, yet one we find to be quite joyful because it is a teaching day of welcoming, taking time to talk with families, and preparing foods that we make with the children for our family-style meals. The transition teacher experiences a strong sense of purpose and satisfaction in caring for the community at large and for each teacher.

This happens in the same way that choosing to participate in daily rituals, like cooking and setting the table for lunch, provides a feeling of caring and pride about contributing to the community for each child.

I am learning that the intentional informality and flexibility of our program over all these years corresponds well with how we live outside in the big world. For example, our morning (8:30–10:30 a.m. or so) and afternoon snacks (around 3:00 p.m. onward) are offered to children as they are hungry. Children convene around our kitchen table in small groups. Sometimes children like to dine alone, other times children cozy up and share their seats to make room for more friends, and sometimes they have to wait for a spot. Lunch is the only time in our day when we schedule everyone to sit together much like a family dinner. The conversations are lively. We reflect on all the things we did during the morning, we make plans about what we might like to do in the afternoon, we tell knock-knock jokes, or we relax with friends as well as with a few parents who pull up a stool to enjoy a piece of homemade bread before taking their child home after a half-day session.

Because we do not set our day according to the clock, the transition teacher role is very important for a couple of reasons. This teacher sets a general rhythm to the day, not only through a unique welcome but through the ways he or she chooses to get the necessary chores done during the school day. Each teacher has her or his own personal style and rhythm and everyone (staff and children) balances with these differences. This method of engaging in our day and staying organized profoundly influences the culture of our school because it sets the tone for taking care of our basic needs *in relationship with a person*, rather than with a clock. In this way, I have discovered that children do not typically frame their organizational questions according to time (What time is project time? What time is free play? When will it be story time?). Instead, they tend to inquire about projects and people by asking questions and making plans (Who is the kitchen teacher today? I'd like to be a lunch helper. When Dana [the teacher] gets here, I'd like to ask her to do sewing. I'm feeling like doing take apart—can we do that now? Who wants to go outside?). This subtle shift in questioning enables the children to inspire, initiate, and create their day based on their developing repertoire of short- and long-term projects, shared interests, and curiosities with peers and teachers. The time the children spend engaging in their plan is uninterrupted by a clocked itinerary demanding quick closures when perhaps they are only just delving below the surface of their inquiry into a state of *flow* (Csikszentmihalyi 1990). We want to enable as much open time as possible to allow for the emergence of deep, meaningful, and memorable experiences.

So, for example, when four-year-old Justin's schedule of days changed for this school year, he took to calling Tuesday his "Liz Day." By linking Tuesday with a teacher, he created his own method of orientation. Justin attends the center on a part-time basis, and he knows that we are both at Stepping Stones on Tuesdays. So he has expectations about what we will do on those days. I, too, know that I have a learning relationship to uphold with him. Currently we share strong interests in science and photography. So when I arrived at work on the first Tuesday of Justin's schedule change, I was delighted to be met with Justin's provocation, "Liz, I have my science book in my bag. And, guess what? That volcano is *still* in there!"

Just around this same time last year, we were working a lot with clay, and when Justin brought in his science book, we decided to sculpt our first volcano. The project grabbed the attention of many other interested players, and we experimented with the volcano inside the center and then outside in the backyard over the course of two weeks. When we were done, we fed the remaining clay back into the earth. Remembering the adventures of this experience, Justin was inviting me to do it again.

This time, in addition to clay, Justin thought we could use stones, and when other newly interested explorers joined in, our ideas grew and we decided to collect more natural materials from the backyard (leaves, sticks, and mulch). It was September and new children were learning about how the day flows, how they could belong and contribute to the community, and how they could take charge in shaping their day. What better way to learn about your membership in a new place than engaging in a dynamic experiment with an enthusiastic and experienced peer?

▲ Children explore clay with natural materials.

While the provocation was of a scientific nature, it was also an opportunity to develop partnerships. And it created a context for discovering that "My friends and I can be innovators and meaning-makers together" because children learn by doing. By the time the volcano was constructed, not only did the children move on to conduct and observe a science experiment as a small group, they also learned about each other's interests and skills and shared their unique knowledge and even their personal stories with the group. One child talked about a volcano book that she could bring in, another shared about making a volcano with his dad, and Justin and I talked about the volcano we made last year. The investigation required children to work in close proximity to one another, to take turns, and to be flexible with how things unfold with many hands at play.

Even cleaning up, at which time the children invented a new game of jumping on the clay, brought an unexpected energy and learning experience that delayed my plans to invite them to draw and reflect on their observations. It was a moment in which I had reached a crossroads. Do I insist on following through with my teacher expectation of children writing and documenting, or do I support their desire to embrace their own inventiveness by playing a new game? Both were important processes.

Being the start of a new school year, camaraderie and solidarity won out and we dragged the tablecloth and block of clay into our large block room where there would be plenty of space to run and jump on the clay safely. In this gross-motor play, children learned to appreciate each others' physical efforts, take turns, learn each others' names as I called their turn, and create their own challenges like jumping high and hard enough to make the clay snap. I expect we will erupt the volcano many more times in the coming days and will have plenty of opportunity to reflect on our experience, and it will be worth the wait.

▲ Children explore clay with joy and exuberance.

The Children's Tradition: Tea and Stories

There is an aspect of this center that commands attention, and that is the previously mentioned culture of creativity. Liz explains that at Stepping Stones the teachers are supported and encouraged in their creativity and can function according to their interests. They have the freedom to bring their whole selves into the school rather than the expectation to "behave like a teacher." When teachers have the freedom to explore items of interest they can be responsive, pay attention and listen, and act accordingly. For example, in Liz's case, she was able to develop a treasured event called "Tea and Stories."

Tea and Stories is a time developed due to Liz's own interest in bringing relationships to the forefront of curriculum. Liz recognized that when people, whether adults or children, sit around in a relaxed and respectful environment they are able to tell their stories. These stories could be about anything at all—their families, experiences, made-up tales, responses to events, ideas, and so on. Often, when adults sit around and talk, they drink tea or some other beverage or they eat together.

▲ Tea and Stories.

Wanting to recreate this atmosphere of listening for the children, Liz invented Tea and Stories, a time when any child or children could sit with a teacher in a cozy and safe atmosphere and tell stories. The children clearly love this tradition, and it has been a part of the school for some years. When a child commented "we haven't had Tea and Stories for a while," Liz was quick to respond, and several children joined her at a table in the library that morning.

Charlie, however, did not join in. Sitting on a futon nearby, he could hear the stories being told but chose not to join the group. He was experimenting with his fingers, making a kind of mask over his eyes, and yet Liz sensed he was listening to what was going on. Eventually, when there was a break in the conversation, Charlie stood up on the couch and showed the other children what he had been doing. They listened with interest and then continued with their stories. Charlie remained standing at the table of storytellers listening in on the chat, and Liz responded to Charlie's presence by saying, "You know, you told us a kind of story by describing how to make a mask with your hands." Charlie smiled and said, "I know how to do other tricks with my hands too. Do you want to see?" Like a contagious round of knock-knock jokes, children practiced and shared a variety of finger tricks and even some yoga moves.

▲ Children demonstrate hand tricks.

When Tea and Stories was finished, Liz approached Charlie and asked if he would like to write down the directions for how he created masks with his fingers, and he liked this idea very much. Liz helped him to write this first small book, which was later shared with others and then placed on the classroom bookshelf. Liz said, "A significant affirmation of Charlie's efforts occurred when Lucy, a four-year-old, took interest in his writing and asked if she could read it aloud. Charlie was not quite reading yet, but Lucy was unusually skilled and thirsty for a try. Imagine the impact of this exchange on each of these children. The author heard his book read aloud by his peer. Charlie went on to write many 'how to' books, all of which are enjoyed by other children and have inspired them to write their own 'how to' books as well. As a result of this work, my coteachers and I are constantly seeking ways to enable children to be resources for one another."

▲ A child writes and illustrates a how-to book.

This brief example illustrates how listening, paying attention, and responding—in this case to an individual child—has a huge effect on what happens next and on how the child benefits. In this case, since Liz was in conversation with a larger group of children, it would have been easy to overlook the actions of Charlie when he chose not to tell stories to the group. Liz's recognition that he did in fact share something of himself, in the form of demonstrating what he'd been doing, allowed her to follow up on his actions. It also allowed Charlie to develop his writing skills by making a book about his idea. The many books Charlie made provided him with a more comfortable outlet than verbally sharing his stories.

In a setting such as Stepping Stones, there is freedom to pay attention to these seemingly small events. If, for example, Liz worked in a classroom with time frames that demanded she immediately move into another activity after Tea and Stories, she would not have been free to pursue this work with Charlie. In some cases, once the moment is past, it is lost in terms of the interest of the child.

Another emergent curriculum aspect of this school is the time provided for meetings and discussion. Each week, teachers have an hour and a half to write in the journals they keep for each child. In addition, each teacher has an hour to themselves for reflection and planning. Another hour a week is reserved for "dialogue time," in which two teachers at a time are able to leave the floor to discuss and develop shared projects. Once a month, the center closes early and the whole staff comes together for a meeting with an agenda, which includes sharing and discussion.

But aside from these formal arrangements, there are also informal discussions all the time. These take place over coffee or during the workday. The teachers chat together about questions that have arisen for them or a response, or they compare notes or ask "what if?" These informal dialogues might then be taken to a dialogue meeting where ideas can be "brainstormed out" a little. This is quite unstructured but provides food for thought and reflection afterward. Depending on what happens during the brainstorming and reflection, there may be a plan for the next day—something to try—or perhaps a plan will be made *with* the child. When teachers have freedom in terms of what they are able to bring to the classroom, the curriculum itself becomes a wonderful collaboration, a mix of both children's and teachers' interests and needs. The relationships become authentic, and the curriculum becomes relationship-based.

Tea and Stories is not a typical part of an early childhood daily routine nor is the role of transition teacher. You probably won't find these approaches described in Early Childhood Education (ECE) curriculum books or college courses. They were developed from a place of creativity in response to children and the creative, responsive teachers who collaborate with them, and so they work for all the protagonists.

The next chapter includes a story about teachers who rethink routines for toddlers, especially in the sense of where curriculum happens. The story inspires us to think creatively not only about planned activities and routines but also about where these take place.

7

Emergent Curriculum with Toddlers

The importance of listening and observing is connected with the spirit of transition, which cannot be defined with a precise beginning and a precise end. It is a period in which there are pauses, times when we try something, then adjust the situation, while continually involving the parents and their thoughts.

—Cristina Bondavalli

Teachers who work with toddlers have many questions about emergent curriculum. How can curriculum unfold when toddlers' interests may change within seconds? How can we use all the extraordinary moments that occur during the toddler day and respond to their quickly changing needs?

Toddlers and Extraordinary Moments

Sometimes the nature of a toddler's work in the classroom seems to be fleeting—a quick, yet very intense interest in a material or play scenario and then a move to something equally intriguing to the child. The environment, therefore, is incredibly important for a toddler because this child is the epitome of an active learner. The toddler must be able to handle materials, have room to move, create messes with wonderful sensory materials, climb, and use her body in rambunctious ways. In other words, toddlers' minds and bodies are fully engaged with exploration and learning.

When using emergent curriculum with toddlers, we have the choice of using these quick, engaging moments as a starting point for program development or using them as an impetus for changing the environment in response to the toddler's needs. Either way, because toddlers are often not able to articulate their interests as older children do, the educator must be especially astute in observing and responding.

Toddlers can indeed be engaged in projects, but the projects may not resemble those of a preschool group. Instead, toddler teachers practicing emergent curriculum find themselves exploring more global agendas, such as being in a group, finding out about the outdoors, delving into new materials, exploring ideas of independence and interdependence, or spending weeks being immersed (quite literally) in sensory experiences.

There are two groups of toddlers featured in this chapter, one in Canada and one in the United States. The stories illustrate how their teachers responded to their needs, in one case with a change in environment and in the other with responsiveness to the children's need to communicate with their parents.

Andrea's Story: Taking the Classroom Outdoors

Toddlers are unique in terms of their needs. Caught between the quest for increasing independence and the continual need for nurturing, they can be in turn delightful, fiery, loving, determined, knowledgeable, endlessly curious, and perplexing—all in the space of an hour.

For toddlers, having to separate from their family on arrival at child care can be an especially difficult time. Andrea Foster, who works with toddlers in the Family

Room at the Child and Family Development Center (CFDC) in Concord, New Hampshire, wanted to make arrival time easier for the toddlers in her care and also for their parents.

At the same time, she had noticed that the beautiful natural outdoor space at the CFDC was somewhat underused. As with many child care centers, time spent outdoors was only during "outside time." Although the children adored this time outdoors, it was fairly restricted in terms of children's choices about when to go out and when to return indoors. The daily routine, which was developed by teachers, was split into typical time frames that included all the usual components of a toddler day, including a specific time frame for being outside.

Andrea, along with her colleagues, reflected on how these two challenges—toddler arrival and the use of the outdoors—could dovetail. The teachers wanted to give the children more choices about the outdoors, particularly in terms of more time, and wondered whether being dropped off outdoors would make a difference in how the toddlers felt about their parents leaving. After much reflection and dialogue, the team decided to try moving the bulk of the toddlers' days, even in inclement weather, outdoors. They would attempt to develop an outdoor curriculum and see what would happen.

It is easy to imagine that this move felt somewhat risky to the teachers. New Hampshire weather can be severe in winter, and there is lots of time involved with dressing and undressing very young children (yet with arrival taking place outdoors, this quickly became a nonissue). How would the parents feel about this? At first, Andrea reported, parents were divided in their reactions to the idea of the majority of the day being spent outdoors. Some embraced the idea, while others wondered about children with colds or asthma being outdoors. With much dialogue focused on the children's needs and with time, parents embraced the program, and newcomers to the CFDC now enter this toddler environment with excitement.

The toddler teachers begin each day by hauling some of the indoor furniture to the outside space. This requires extra sacrifice on the part of staff because only one teacher is available on the first shift of the day and that teacher arrives earlier than what would be normally required. The moving of shelves and large baskets is no small task. But doing this has

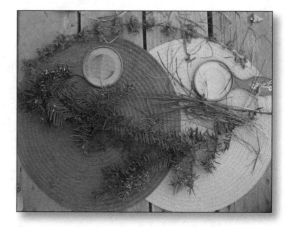

▲ A beautiful invitation to explore magnifying glasses and natural materials.

enabled the teachers to create an outdoor classroom. In addition to the natural earth berms, amphitheater, sandbox, and winding paths, the outdoor classroom also includes a reading area, blocks on a platform, a sensory table, and anything else that, according to their observations, the teachers feel is necessary.

▲ An inviting area for reading outdoors.

The children now spend almost their entire day outdoors. Once the second teacher has arrived, the children are free to choose whether they stay outside or move inside. For the most part, the children choose to stay outside.

WORTH THE EXTRA WORK

Is the extra work worth the effort? Does learning outdoors differ from learning indoors? Andrea reported that the outdoor explorations could be extremely engaging for children who normally have a short attention span. For example, she observed a toddler exploring shadows who for an hour was completely focused on observing the shadow, touching it, moving around it, and stepping onto it and then repeating the whole process.

The toddlers' endless need for physical action was also addressed. They now nap well and eat well. When the children simply need to wander, this is no longer the challenge it can be indoors where space is more limited and children tend to crowd each other. Andrea believed fewer social challenges occurred and less guidance was needed since self-regulation seemed to develop more naturally outdoors. When the children do venture indoors, they use the indoor materials in a more focused way, as if they are seeing them through fresh eyes.

The outdoors has endless opportunities for creative thinking and responses for both children and adults. Many of the materials—sand, earth, water, and pebbles—are open-ended and continuous (that is, they move and change shape) rather than static. This opens up many more possibilities for the child. Outside, mess simply doesn't matter. With what amounts to a doubled play space that uses the outdoors as much as the indoors, easier social relationships, and more allowances for independent choices, both toddlers and teachers enjoy this flexible and joyful space.

The teachers in this team are committed to what works best for the children. So often we restrict ourselves to what has been done before, to what is efficient in terms of time and effort, or to some other perception of how an early childhood routine should be. Breaking out of these old scripts instead requires a disposition of openness, willingness to try something unusual, and the ability to ask ourselves "what if?"

An account of another toddler classroom in which the teacher had to think about a new approach to a familiar challenge follows.

Shannon's Story: Connecting Toddlers with Their Parents at Work

Shannon Harrison returned to the classroom to work with young children after a period of five years as an early childhood consultant. At Point Pleasant Child Care Centre in Halifax, Nova Scotia, Shannon began working with a group of toddlers between the ages of eighteen months and three years.

Point Pleasant is a large organization licensed for 122 children in three urban settings. The children and their families are from diverse backgrounds, as are the teachers. All of the teachers are experienced early childhood educators, and the retention of staff is impressive. The organization is committed to working with emergent approaches; therefore, the executive director, Susan Willis, has for some time provided continuous support for staff in the form of a part-time consultant who supports teachers through dialogue, documentation support, regular retreats, and workshops.

Having worked as a consultant herself, Shannon knew what practices should be part of her day. While forming relationships with her group of children over the first few months, she watched carefully, supported toddlers in their journey toward independence, and adjusted the environment to suit their needs.

The toddler classroom is a bright and spacious place situated at the end of a long hallway. At the other end of the hallway is the kitchen and the center's full-time cook, Draga. As Shannon watched the daily life of toddlers unfold, she also noticed that due to the position of the classroom in the facility, the children had no idea where their food actually came from. It was as if their lunch magically appeared from nowhere, and they had no contact with Draga, one of the most important people in the center. Shannon decided on a goal of "making it real" for the toddlers; that is, she would help them understand their immediate community and all the

 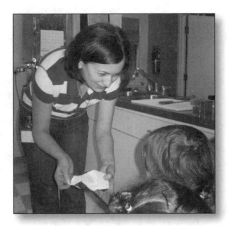

▲ Toddlers arrive in the kitchen to meet the cook.

people in it. With this in mind, the toddlers and their teachers visited the kitchen and came to know the cook and her name.

At this point, a new child joined the class. As with many children this age, the child had some difficulty with separation and was often told by teachers that "Mommy is at work." When Shannon thought about these words, however, some questions came up. In terms of making it real, Shannon wondered what those words actually meant, if anything at all, to the children. What exactly do children know about their parents' workplaces and what they do there?

The team decided to send a digital camera home with the children's families. This was a challenge, since they had to obtain a camera at low cost or by donation. Through research and scouring of online sources, a camera at an affordable price was found.

Teachers asked adult family members to have photos of themselves taken by a coworker as they did their jobs. This endeavor took a long time to organize. With only one camera available and families keeping the camera for a few days before returning it, it took several weeks to collect photos of all the adults in their work- places. Along with the camera went a set of instructions. Shannon wanted the photos to show the adults in action rather than looking at the camera or posing. She felt this would provide the children with a realistic idea of what their adult family members actually did and provide the teachers with some information they could discuss with the children.

As the photos trickled in, children saw their family members teaching a class full of children at school, working at a computer or in a lab, sculpting a piece of art, and taking courses at a university. There were also photos of people working on the phone or at a desk, such as an accountant, a human resources manager, an office administrator, and a university professor.

The photos were assembled into a binder that was placed where children could easily reach it. The children looked at the binder often. Shannon believes that the photos, in addition to making the phrase "Mommy is at work" more meaningful for the children, are comforting for them. These images help to bridge the gap between child care and workplace, and the families also enjoy this aspect of the program.

While it is true that many groups of children are able to visit adult family members in the workplace, this isn't the case for everyone due to geography, transportation issues, or workplace regulations. In this case, the use of photography

▲ Children examine photos of their parents at work.

served its purpose, and the children had a reference point for *work*. By thinking of all the possibilities and not being daunted by the challenges, the teachers were able to "make it real" for these toddlers.

Responsiveness to children and their needs does not always have to be in the form of activities or materials. For young children, routines, relationships, and physical environments are often the crux of their program. They need psychological safety and a program specifically attuned to them. When we watch, listen, and think of all the possibilities, we are more likely to create a toddler-centered program that works for the children and their families and, therefore, works for the teachers as well.

Connecting children with their families is important. So is connecting families with their children and the school or child care program. One of the most powerful tools for communication between teachers and families is documentation in its many forms. The next chapter examines program plans and other forms of communication proven to be meaningful and accessible for everyone involved.

8

The Challenge
of Documenting
Emergent Curriculum

**An emergent curriculum is a continuous revision process, an honest
response to what is actually happening. Good teachers *plan and let go*.
If you're paying attention to children, an accurate lesson plan can be
written only after the fact. It is important to be accountable for what
really happens, as distinguished from one's intentions. Teachers are
often hoodwinked by their good intentions.**

—ELIZABETH JONES AND JOHN NIMMO

In previous chapters, the stories have been about responsive and creative teaching.
Some teachers were able to respond to unusual tangents, such as Michelle's experience with the hockey players and issues of power and strength. Others demonstrated
flexibility in scheduling or routines, such as Liz with Tea and Stories or Andrea who
took her curriculum outdoors to suit the needs of the children, which is needed for
curriculum to emerge.

We early childhood practitioners know that extraordinary moments occur throughout each teaching day. Many of these moments and the responses to them are never recorded. Sometimes this is simply because there are too many of them, and we cannot record absolutely everything. At other times, it is difficult to find a format that works with the flexibility and innovation of emergent curriculum.

Given the need for accountability to our licensing bodies, boards of directors, families, and supervisors, how do we write down what is happening within the dynamic and changing environment that is commonplace when using this approach? The typical planning form or book full of pages to fill in, activities to plan in advance, and units to be outlined does not work well for us. Teachers have used many formats to make an emergent curriculum visible to others. Here are some that worked well as well as some that were not as successful.

Naomi's Journal

I have to laugh at myself sometimes when I realize how much of a natural planner and organizer I am and how completely different following an emergent curriculum can be. It has been a real challenge figuring out the process of planning. It is exhausting trying to jump into emergent curriculum with both feet—learning the process, the language; trying to develop the art of questioning, observing, documenting . . . and at the end of the day chewing over what I've seen that day to figure out where to go with planning for tomorrow in a manner that is inquiry-based.

Organized, Tidy, and Never Used

The typical planning sheet in an early childhood setting, if indeed there is such a thing, often has sections based on the daily routine of the classroom, such as circle time, play centers, and small-group time. Or the planning sheet may have sections for each area of the classroom, such as construction, drama, and art areas. The task of the teacher is to fill in the boxes. The problem with this approach, however, is the sheet cannot show the thinking behind the plans, the recording of children's questions and interests, or the teacher's responses to observations.

This type of planning sheet is more left-brained, or organized, tidy, and sometimes not followed. There are myriad unexpected happenings in an early childhood classroom that a responsive teacher simply cannot ignore. Consider, for example, the intriguing items children bring in from home or the outdoors or the thought-provoking questions that arise out of a project the children are working on. How can these be incorporated onto a sheet designed to outline activities or centers in advance? This type of planning sheet is more suited to events that happen in lockstep or a linear and predictable fashion. It does not allow for creative thinking on the part of the teacher or for recording innovative thoughts and ideas from children.

Naomi's Journal

It seems I've been spending a lot of time lately trying to create a planning template that will be useful when working with emergent curriculum. It is so important to have a planning template that allows me to see the interests and topics emerging and progressing from day to day and week to week. Originally I was using the same daily planning sheet I used last year, with the day broken down into time and subject slots, but I've quickly realized that I'm missing such a key ingredient in my planning. I was starting to feel like things were disjointed because I was unable to easily see the flow and progression over time. The big difference with emergent curriculum versus using a premade curriculum is that when you use a prepackaged program, a building of skills and ideas is already factored in. You can usually trust the program to factor in how to make each day and week flow smoothly. Emergent curriculum allows you to bring nothing to the table except your daily observations, therefore you need to be able to easily see the emerging ideas, interests, and learning that is taking place or else you will miss so much!

My newest template allows me to see a week's worth of planning for the centers I am responsible for, my small group, the afternoon literature, and science. This has enabled me to see all of my daily responsibilities at a quick glance and whether or not I have flow throughout the day within each area of my responsibilities. It also enables me to see what is happening from day to day in each area. I can see how I've built on the previous day in my small group, science, and so forth.

Linking Observations to Curriculum

Over the years, the early childhood professionals I have collaborated with in various settings have grappled with this dilemma. Together we have designed and field-tested many types of formats for recording curriculum, including curriculum paths and webs, double-sided pages that allow for more writing, and simple three-column formats that attempt to show the spiraling nature of emergent curriculum. None of these were completely satisfying, although some have worked better than others. I present samples of these formats here, for your consideration, so that they might spark some ideas for your own program.

When attempting to demonstrate how emergent curriculum is evolving, it is helpful to show how your observations have led to curriculum. Although observations of specific children must be kept confidential, it is possible to share a generalized summary of what the observations of children's play have been demonstrating so that families and others can see curriculum is being developed from this source. Therefore, you may want a documentation format with space for a brief summary of observations, the response (what you intend to try in terms of questions, conversations, invitations, or changes to the environment), and follow-up observations to show the circular nature of planning.

In some settings, we have tried a four-column format. The observation in the fourth column of this format becomes a starting point for the next reflection and response. The challenge with this approach is that the responses (in the third column) will probably be in several forms—changes to environment, questions to pose, activities to invite children to explore, and so on—so the chart must have room for all of these.

Observation	Teacher's Reflection	Response: Invitations, Conversations, Activities, Projects	Follow-up Observation

A similar format was implemented at another location using one of these charts for every area of the classroom, such as sensory, writing, and construction. A different member of the team was responsible for observing and responding in each of these areas as well as for completing the documentation for that area. Teacher-led activities, such as morning meetings, or small-group times, were planned on a separate paper. Although this approach worked quite well, it was time-consuming and created a great deal of paperwork to be organized and stored.

If you imagine reading through the following chart, you can see in your mind's eye that there is, in fact, a zigzag or spiraling pattern from observation to response and back to observation again. Over time, when reflecting on previous plans, you may even see a revisiting or repetition of an idea in children's play or in teachers' responses, in which the spiraling nature of emergent curriculum again becomes evident.

Classroom area: Observations, Science, and Construction areas　　**Week of:** May 10–14

Observer: Susan

Monday	Tuesday	Wednesday	Thursday	Friday
Responses / Plans	*Responses / Plans*	*Responses / Plans*	*Responses / Plans*	*Responses / Plans*
In response to previous work on movement, let's try experimenting with the movement/pathway of light: · flashlights · variety of paper · mirrors	Continue to experiment with mirrors. Support children's efforts to find random objects to shine light through. Create own patterns with paper to shine light through.	In response to a meeting-time discussion about the transfer of energy, let's try using pendulums with globes and apples to try to figure out how energy is moving the objects.	Make Newton's Cradle available for experimentation.	
Observations	*Observations*	*Observations*	*Observations*	*Observations*
Children were able to quite accurately predict where light would go. Sarah picked out random objects to shine light through. Children were a little confused by the rebound of light from mirrors.	Children were very interested in using scissors to create shapes and used the shapes effectively with flashlight. Children referred to the shapes that reflected onto the wall as "fish shapes."	Children seemed to come up with a theory of how energy transfers from one thing to another.	Amazement and confusion! Children were surprised to see the speed of the ball movement change with the number of balls that were moving.	

Classroom area: <u>Observations, Science, and Construction areas</u>   Week of: <u>May 3-7</u>

Observer: <u>Janet</u>

MONDAY	TUESDAY	WEDNESDAY	THURSDAY	FRIDAY
Responses / Plans	*Responses / Plans*	*Responses / Plans*	*Responses / Plans*	*Responses / Plans*
Invite children to set up two different surfaces, bumpy and smooth, for experimentation.	Provide an inclined plane to experiment with how vehicles move on/up/down a slope.	Invite children to move cars and trucks up the ramp using a weight and pulley system.	Construct pulley systems. Encourage children to attach their own items to the pulley.	Invite children to make simple cars.
Observations	*Observations*	*Observations*	*Observations*	*Observations*
Children enjoyed pushing cars over a bumpy surface. They looked in truck books to compare different wheel sizes.	Children raced different sized cars and found that heavier ones moved faster. They added height to the ramp. They added speed bumps. They added weight to one car and guessed correctly that this one would move faster.	Children enjoyed guessing how many rocks it would take to move the weight up. They understood that the steeper the hill, the more weight it would take.	The children really enjoyed making pulleys. They were able to work very independently on these.	Using a variety of materials (twigs for axels, buttons for wheels) and with some teacher support, children were able to construct simple cars that they tested on the ramps.

My team and I have been working with a format that has room for a summary of observations, plans for what will happen the next day, and teachers responsible for working with each group of children or project. Specific observations of children are stored separately and away from the public eye since they contain names; however, they could be made available when licensing officials visit the school. Since there is a great deal of information on this sheet, we have formatted it with a landscape orientation and fold it when it is placed in a binder for storage.

Transparency -1
beginning Sept 1

Trans -2

First intro to watercolour paint

watercolours: mixing of shades (studio)

(obs) "I can see through that!"

(early Sept) general exploration of water during play

(provocation) Addition of trans. objects and tools

(Sept 11) Continuation of exploration, with addition of light

(15th)
- Sorting according to colour/shadow or no colour/shadow
- Art on acetates w/projector
- using water + light in water tables to compare transp./non-transp

Several water centres w/ trans. objects in response to intense interest

Invitation: Overhead projector and variety of papers (see-through or not?)

watercolours vs tempera (explore transparency of each)

(Sept 17th)
→ further exploring and defining terms "clear" and "transparent"
→ Provocations:
  - where does the light beam go? (Experiment w/flashlt)
  - What if you were invisible for a day?

"Emperor's New Clothes"

draw self & trace onto transparency

(Sept 21st)
→ Placed transp. "windows" in doll house

Obs: "Hey! I've found something I can see through it!"

▲ A curriculum path.

Showing the Curriculum over the Long Term

When reflecting on your curriculum, it is helpful to examine what has happened over the long term—in recent weeks or months. While you can, of course, go to a storage system or binder and examine daily pages, it is helpful to have an at-a-glance format that outlines the broad categories of children's interests, follow-up investigations they were engaged in, and tangents that flowed from this into other projects.

This kind of curriculum path makes our long-term journey with children visible and can also be used to revisit the journey with the children themselves. They are often impressed and excited about how much they have done. Teachers who are feeling a little lost as to where they are in their own journey with emergent curriculum are reassured when they see the journey outlined. The curriculum path can also help teachers articulate to others how an investigation unfolded, complete with all its twists and turns.

Above is an example of a recent curriculum path from the four- and five-year-old classroom at Halifax Grammar School.

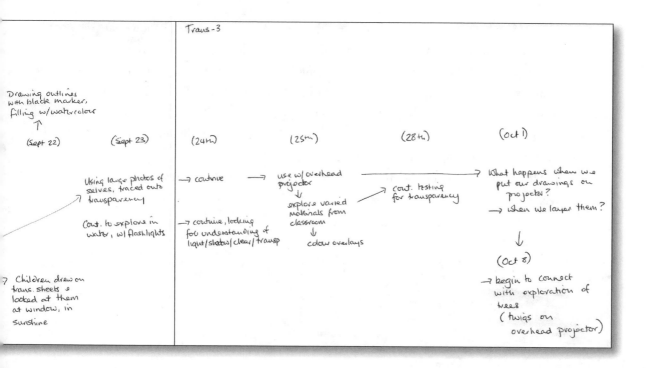

Brainstorming with a Web

Webbing was a popular form of planning some years ago and, in terms of brainstorming, can still be a useful tool. When we let ideas flow while meeting with colleagues and then organize these ideas into a web, it allows for unexpected events to be added and tangents to be followed.

For example, when a group of children are interested in the ocean, this might veer off in the direction of ships, fish, pirates, treasure maps, or something altogether unexpected. Whatever the children's thinking or questions, they can be added to a web and new webs can be formed from these tangents.

As ideas and interests arise, they can be coded to identify whether the idea is the child's, the teacher's, or a collaboration between the two. This is easily done by using different colored pens to write each of the protagonists' ideas or to draw around the ideas of children with one color and the teachers' ideas with another. In these ways, the "weight" of the investigation is visible; that is, it becomes easy to see whether or not there is shared decision making within the classroom—whether the direction of the program is a true collaborative effort or is teacher-dominated.

There is also a true feeling of flow when questions and ideas are simply noted on a web rather than entered into the somewhat official format of filling in boxes on a planning sheet. There is something about completing empty boxes that is mind-numbing. A free-form curriculum web might be a way of releasing ideas and getting them down on paper as a *possibility* rather than a *commitment*. When the possibility does in fact become an activity or event, then it is noted, which should satisfy licensing representatives or administrators.

Here is an example of how an interest in a tree house might be represented by a web.

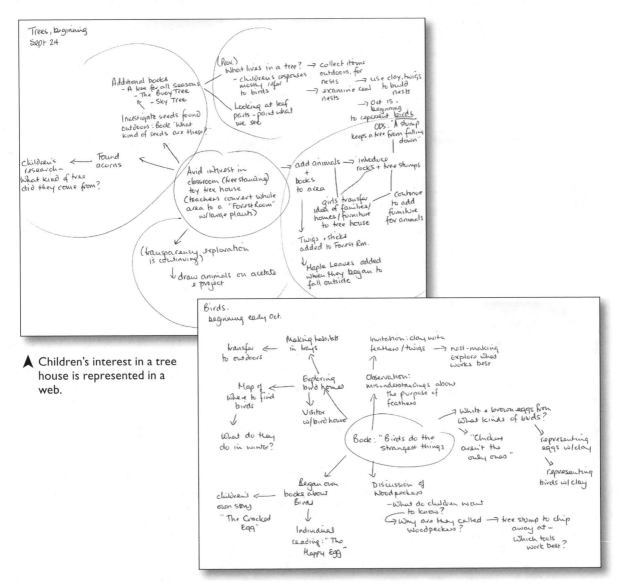

▲ Children's interest in a tree house is represented in a web.

▲ The children's responses to "What lives in a tree?" mainly centered around birds, which led to a deeper investigation of birds and their habitats.

We could not have imagined from observing play at the tree house that so many investigations would follow. So much was happening—often at the same time—that it was extremely helpful to see the work and its tangents all in one place.

When we are not confined to boxes, then creativity has a chance to flourish. We do not feel the pressure to complete something by filling in a form; instead, we can make visible the journey we are taking with the children. The children can see it, too, and if the webs or curriculum paths are supported by visual documentation, they can easily revisit and remember their important work.

Documentation Is the Story of What Happened

Our counterparts in Reggio Emilia have done us a great service by providing examples of how visual documentation of children's work can be meaningful and resonate deeply with those who see it, while being aesthetically stunning.

Many educators in North America and other places outside of northern Italy are using this type of pedagogical documentation on a regular basis and finding it invaluable in terms of telling the story of children's work and sharing it with others in the school, community, and field of early education.

Although it may be presented in different design formats, usually there is photographic evidence of the project, traces of the children's work, and perhaps samples of pertinent dialogue. Some people include the teachers' own reflections and resulting questions as well.

The following examples of photographic documentation tell the story of "how it works."

During the tree project, children began to think about the tree as a home. They focused on birds, and their first drawings were simple and fairly stereotypical.

▲ Day after day, the children chose to draw birds and used books, models, and real birds outdoors as references. Slowly their drawings became more sophisticated. These drawings were produced approximately two weeks after the first ones. ➤

◄ As the children thought about and examined nests, they collected materials from outdoors to experiment with. Using them on the overhead projector, they began to think about how birds could join these materials together.

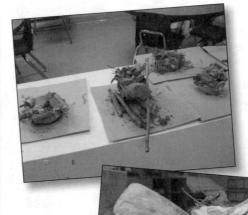

The teachers offered clay as an invitation, along with the natural materials from outdoors. Over a period of days in small groups during play, the children experimented with making nests.

Their comfort with clay afforded children the opportunity to make birds. Noah had looked at many books about birds and also possessed much prior knowledge, since he had watched birds with his family outdoors. These models were made over a period of days. Note the detail of the crest on the blue jay!

◄ The study of birds led to thinking about what they might eat and how they would obtain that food. After discussing why a woodpecker pecks at trees, Naomi extended another invitation by providing tree trunks. The children did some research on the best tools for digging holes in the trunks. Wearing goggles, they experimented with many objects and found that golf tees worked quite well as bug hunters. The children, after much persistence, did actually find a live bug within the tree trunk. They commented on how hard the woodpecker's beak must be to do such hard work.

Documentation of this kind provides an opportunity to reflect deeply about the work as we put it all together with our team members, program coordinator, or director. It validates our important work by explaining the intense thought behind what we do. It is time-consuming but worthwhile as a tool for communication, children's learning, and teachers' professional growth.

Trying different ways of planning and documenting requires the support of other professionals in your organization or perhaps some extra professional development. It also requires a change in mind-set on the part of training programs for early childhood educators.

In the past, many ECE training programs were influenced by the way elementary schools plan their daily events with children, but there has been a shift in that thinking. For example, in Canada and the United States there are teacher educators and college administrators trying new ways of educating teachers that reflect the early childhood field and philosophies, which are quite different from the way elementary teachers are trained. The next chapter includes the story of such a program and a person who dared to think differently about how to make ECE philosophies come to life for her adult students.

Supporting the Process: The Role of Teacher Education Programs and Administrators

9

> When we learn to ask good questions, we discover that yet another competence is needed: the ability to turn a question-and-answer session between the teacher and individual students into a complex communal dialogue that bounces all around the room. My students will learn much more when I turn their eyes from always looking at me and help them look at one another.
>
> —PARKER J. PALMER

The insights, innovative practices, and explorations teachers draw from in emergent curriculum do not exist in a vacuum. Behind the scenes are supports for emergent curriculum that make the journey possible and encourage teachers to take risks and think creatively. In this chapter, teacher educators and administrators share their stories about their programs' efforts to promote inquiry, constructivism, promising practices, and innovation.

Hope's Story: Facilitating Loosening Up

Hope Moffatt in Fort McMurray, Alberta, is passionate about teaching and learning with adults. She works not only with student teachers but also with other adults on boards and committees. Usually meetings conducted by boards and committees are rigidly entrenched in the scripts of "how to run a meeting" or "how to come to a decision." In the following example, Hope shares a way of loosening up these scripts.

Hope has found that her other passion—music—has enabled people to think creatively. She believes this is because music hooks into the right side of the brain, allowing people to uncover previously hidden ideas. She offers the following example from serving on a board of directors for a family resource center. The board consisted of eight people and had been in existence for one and a half years.

The board wanted to work on the organization's vision and hired a consultant to help them through this process. In the morning of a full-day session, the consultant did some interesting work with visual images, using magazines and other cues. After lunch, Hope tried something more unusual by leading the group downstairs to a large room, where they formed a circle. She introduced many kinds of drums, and what followed was, in effect, a drumming circle that moved and inspired the group. They drummed together for about half an hour, after which they returned to their meeting. Then, within fifteen minutes, the group developed their vision: honoring children, engaging families, connecting community.

While some participants felt it was the drumming that helped them to create this vision, there were many factors involved. The cohesiveness that resulted from working together and engaging in something unusual and creative, the power of drums (perhaps a feeling of belonging and working together), the break from a typical meeting format that coaxed the right brain to kick into action, and the preceding visualizations likely all played a role. It is interesting that when something like this happens, our left brain asks "why?" rather than simply accepting and enjoying the results!

Meetings, classes, and any routine event can be conducted entirely by rote. Or, we can change the script. Hope's example helps us to see that when we place people in unexpected situations, we help them to see things from a new perspective and to reach understanding through a fresh approach. When people trust their group leader, instructor, or administrator, they will be more willing to try new things to loosen up their thinking and, perhaps, come up with creative innovations.

No matter what our position, who we teach or lead, or what kind of committees we serve on, it is important, especially when things become stale or stalled, to break from routines and consider other approaches to a challenge. The more we break away from typical approaches, the more we open ourselves up to innovative ideas that can move us forward.

Lori's Story: Program Coordinator as Provocateur

Many early childhood programs have only their director, and perhaps an assistant director, to take care of everything from the budget to curriculum to maintenance. Other organizations choose to structure their staff differently to put emphasis where they believe it needs to be. For example, in laboratory schools—settings where student teachers watch, practice, and learn—the emphasis is often on curriculum development. The nature of the laboratory school setting demands approaches that link theory to practice.

The Child and Family Development Center (CFDC) at New Hampshire Technical Institute in Concord, New Hampshire, employs a program coordinator, rather than an assistant director, who works directly with the staff on curriculum development. CFDC uses emergent curriculum, and the theory behind this practice is taught in students' classes when they are not in practicum. One of the goals of CFDC is to make theory visible in classroom practices.

Lori Warner's role as program coordinator is to support staff in their journey with emergent curriculum. She is in the three classrooms (infant, toddler, and preschool) 85 percent of the time, observing, interacting with children, and meeting with staff on a rotating basis in the afternoon. Lori explained that each teaching team is unique, bringing a different dynamic to their work.

What does this role involve, and what does Lori actually do to support the teachers' thinking about curriculum? Lori thinks *with* the teachers as they discuss what has been happening in their classrooms. She brings curiosity and genuine questions to the table, rather than attempting to provide answers. Sometimes this means remaining quiet for a few moments in order for teachers to think. Lori might simply ask "why?" in response to an idea or plan. At other times, the teachers and Lori brainstorm together, generating many ideas and building on each other's thoughts, until they comes up with something that feels right for the particular group of children. Eventually, connections made from children's play, conversations, and questions inform what will happen for the next few days.

One of the challenges during these meetings is for teachers to leave their obligations behind and give themselves permission to spend time thinking and talking together, discussing possibilities, and searching for answers. Many teachers are only used to doing this alone and on their own time. To be given time for dialogue is a rare luxury in the field of early childhood education. Lori tries to help teachers focus on the dialogue rather than all the other routine tasks they have to fit in a day. Even twenty minutes of discussion can be tremendously helpful.

Lori also fills the role of a documenter. Documentation is an important tool not only for communication between home and school but also in the school itself. Educators need to share their work with each other in order to create discussion points from which to grow. Finding the time to produce documentation and to read about others' work can be a huge challenge. Lori found that even though she had time outside the classroom to produce documentation for each teaching team, which often served double-duty as a communication tool with families, she could not keep up with the huge amount of information coming to her for sharing. If she spent too much time preparing documentation, she was not able to get into classrooms or meet with teachers. If the documentation was not produced, however, there would be nothing to refer to for reflection with colleagues, children, and parents. Compounding this problem was the fact that many families simply didn't have time to read documentation at the end of the day. While teachers had the opportunity throughout their work day to peruse documentation on the walls and in classroom logs, it was more challenging for family members, who felt rushed with the responsibilities of playtime, suppertime, and bedtime at home.

Lori decided to simply ask a parent who was also a teacher at the center what would make it easier for her to read documentation. The answer was to send it home or to the office by e-mail so parents could read it at their leisure. This idea appealed to Lori, and she began to produce e-documentation weekly. A page of documentation, with photographs embedded, goes home once a week to parents of children in each classroom. This is time efficient for Lori and, more important, her documentation is being more widely read by and producing positive feedback from families.

Curriculum Connection: Toddlers 5/11–5/15

You've Got Mail!

Receiving their own mail at home *did* help to make "mailing" more tangible! Throughout the week, Miss Stephanie engaged in many conversations with children to get a better sense of their understanding of sending and receiving mail. When she repeated the opportunity for children to create a "letter" and mail it home, she observed that the children wanted to recreate their letter exactly. They chose the same color of paper and even recalled their previous intentions and tried to recreate them as well.

Repetition is crucial in child development. Children are always on a quest to master one milestone or another; whether it's climbing stairs or pedaling and steering a bike, control only comes with much practice. Each time a child repeats something familiar, it deepens their understanding and challenges them to rethink their prior understanding of possibilities.

Letter Recognition

Observation: From the envelope/stationary invitation, Hunter borrowed a pen and wrote an "H" in the sand. This shows Hunter has prior experience with and knowledge about the first letter of his name. Recognizing the importance of this literacy development and that it is an obvious source of interest, Miss Jess has created photo name cards for children to explore and use in meaningful ways!

Family Connection

- Repeat successful experiences many times.
- His/her name is an important and meaningful word in a child's life. Rather than expecting children to memorize individual letters of the alphabet, help them to recognize the first letter in their own name; the rest will come through curiosity and exposure.
- Look for familiar letters when you're out and about!

The center's goal for documentation is to illustrate the complexity of emergent curriculum and the collaborative thinking that goes into this approach. When the process of documentation slowed down somewhat, with one sheet per week for each classroom, Lori was able to look for a curriculum thread to focus on, gain input from the teachers, and then make the documentation visible for families.

For Lori and the CFDC staff, thinking together, responding to children, and then illustrating collaboration through documentation have been the key to connecting emergent curriculum with families. Using today's technology to facilitate this process was a creative and important step in CFDC's journey.

The Nature of Teacher Education

Teacher education programs differ widely in the ways they introduce curriculum approaches and philosophies to student teachers. In colleges, department heads and other administrators expect clearly stated outcomes for adult students, a schedule of classes mapped out well in advance, assignments to prove adults have learned what they were supposed to learn, and exams and essays that demonstrate their knowledge. While all of this advance planning (despite instructors and students not yet meeting, let alone getting to know each other) may work for traditional teacher education programs that promote learning about themes, units, and outcomes, those who teach about emergent curriculum find such expectations and advance planning to be perplexing. How can educators be taught to be flexible, child-centered, and responsive with the young children in their classes if instructors are not modeling the emergent curriculum approach in teacher education?

Some instructors have tackled this dilemma in innovative ways. They use modeling—the "practice what we preach" approach—to empower student teachers to confidently use emergent approaches with young children. This may mean an instructor's classes are based on student-centered approaches so that students can "see" what the instructor is trying to relay. Other teacher educators have taken up new approaches to practicum experiences, rethinking their previous scripts for what student teachers actually do in practice and how they do it. Hope Moffatt, the instigator of the drumming circle, has experience taking a playful approach in one of her classes.

Hope teaches at a community college in Fort McMurray, Alberta. She wants her adult students to see possibilities when observing and thinking about young children and to nurture rather than stifle creativity in their classrooms. Hope sees creativity as being linked to resourcefulness. She believes that when students recognize the possibilities and opportunities that come out of children's thinking and play they are able to be more resourceful in terms of what might happen next.

Once when Hope wanted one of her classes to understand the difference between teacher-directed and child-centered activities, she found that art provided a way for students to understand the effects of teacher dominion in a concrete way. One day she arrived at her class in character as "Miss Moffatt." Rather than being her warm and flexible self, Hope became stern and required students to follow instructions instead of their own inclinations during an art project. Then, in contrast, they tried the activity again with no expectations. Students used the materials in any way they wanted without input from the instructor, except for some encouraging support and feedback.

Afterward, when Hope asked the students about the contrasting experiences, they discussed developmentally appropriate practices, the way they had been taught as children, and how it felt to have wonderful materials but no freedom to use them in creative ways. Fifteen years later, Hope met a former student who had been in this class. That student told her that she "wouldn't have understood this in any other way."

Next, another teacher educator shares how she completely rethought her course structure so students could experience the true meaning of using observations to plan curriculum.

Karyn's Story: Teacher Education with a Difference

Karyn Callaghan, professor of early childhood education at Mohawk College in Hamilton, Ontario, has studied the philosophy and practices of Reggio Emilia for many years. Her thinking about Reggio Emilia has influenced the way she approaches her work with adult students of early childhood education. Like many of us who have worked in early childhood education for years, she is also familiar with the work of Lilian Katz, who has pointed out that *how* we are taught is much more influential than *what* we are taught. This idea is particularly important for educators of teachers, since instruction usually includes attempting to bring ideas and experiences that enable adult students to tune in to children's ideas and respond to them. Adult students should experience the benefits of this type of teaching and learning firsthand. Even if "hands-on" learning is involved in a teacher-education class, Karyn realized this may not be enough. If students are learning information the teacher already has in mind (rather than the teacher building on the experiences, questions, and ideas of students), then this approach would not be congruent with the philosophies and approaches the students were learning about in theory. Karyn recognized this dissonance and made the following remarks.

> Coming to this recognition is one thing. Finding ways to achieve congruity in a postsecondary institution is another thing. Colleges are often committed to demonstrating that province or statewide learning outcomes are being met and, so, demand detailed course outlines and assessments. These are to be prepared by the faculty prior to even meeting the students, and it is expected that the students receive them on the first day of class. Schedules are inflexible; classrooms are institutional. There is a hierarchy in these institutions, and issues of power are difficult to confront. There is also a struggle with the traditional view of teachers as the ones with the answers and of teacher educators as the ones who must *really* know the answers. Students of education arrive having been apprentices of education since they entered school as young children and have been influenced by how they have been taught for those years. They are not empty sponges any more than children are. They have strongly held, if usually unarticulated, views of children, teaching, and learning. When first exposed to an alternate way of teaching and learning, students who have learned how to be successful in a traditional school context might feel unsettled. They have been on the receiving end of the transmission model, competing for marks by taking notes, writing tests, and answering questions based on what they infer—or have been told outright—that the teacher wants to hear. Finally, there is the issue of practicum experience, which many believe has an overriding impact on pre-service teachers. Unfortunately, what they learn in some settings is far from ideal. This combination of factors makes for a daunting challenge for those who wish to have a live experience of the Reggio approach with students of education.

When Karyn read Susan Fraser's and Carol Gestwicki's (2002) book, *Authentic Childhood*, she began to see a way out of feeling disconnect in her own courses. In the book, Fraser and Gestwicki describe a project called *Children Teaching Teachers (CTT)*, in which children came to the college classroom to engage in activities planned by the ECE students. The children's work was videotaped and documented by students and reflected on before the children's next visit, with documentation and discussion being used as a basis for planning the next round of activities. The kind of work Fraser and Gestwicki describe is actually a cycle of inquiry that puts into action a process of activity, observation, documentation, reflection, and planning. This cycle seemed to Karyn to be an authentic way for students to experience firsthand a reflective practice built on relationships. When she began to think about how to initiate these kinds of practices at her own college, Karyn recognized the challenges.

> I teach at a college in a large city in southern Ontario. Ours is a two-year program, with approximately 150 students enrolled each year. We were losing our lab school. Our class size ranged from forty-five to fifty, and we were often in classrooms that barely accommodated the number of chairs and tables we needed. We did not have a dedicated classroom exclusively for ECE courses, so when our class time ended a class from another program would be coming in right after. I was passionate about the Reggio Emilia philosophy and had initiated a network of educators in our community who met regularly to discuss how we were making meaning of the approach in our context. I had real life examples to share with the students, but it was not enough. I yearned for a richer experience for them. The logistics of having children come to us were unmanageable, but I thought we could try a flipped-over version of *Children Teaching Teachers* by having our students go out to child care programs in the community instead. I introduced this in the third semester course I teach called Curriculum I. As a faculty, we agreed we wanted the students to gain a deeper understanding of emergent curriculum and had been moving away from a theme-based approach for several years. This course became the place where this would be the focus. The class is scheduled once a week for three hours for fourteen weeks. The students have taken courses in child development, program planning, creative expression, and observation in their first year. The fit of these courses with an emergent approach was not easy and still needed work. But the students showed their ability to modify what they have learned to fit what is needed in this course.

> We spent the first four weeks together in class attempting to unpack those unarticulated views of children, teaching, and curriculum. We watched videos that show a different way of being with children, such as *An Amusement Park for Birds*, the inspiring project filmed in Reggio Emilia; and *To See Takes Time* and *Thinking Big*, filmed

at the Hilltop Children's Center in Seattle, Washington. We read articles about Canadian teachers' experiences as they transform their way of being with children. For years we did not have a text for this course but finally adopted Susan Stacey's *Emergent Curriculum in Early Childhood Settings* and found it to be a perfect fit. The students are intrigued by what they are seeing and reading but are often skeptical it can be brought to life in our context. The major assignment in this course gives them the opportunity to try.

The students form themselves into groups of six, considering their access to helpful resources such as a digital camera, video camera, and transportation. Each group is comprised of two teams of three and assigned to a program that will host their group for the major assignment of the course. The programs asked to play this role have been exploring emergent curriculum and are at different places in their own journey. They see this as an opportunity to enhance their own learning. On week five of the course, the entire class time (9 a.m. to 12 p.m.) is dedicated to a visit to the host program. Permissions are obtained from the parents of children in child care to allow documentation by the students. Ideally, one student in the group is also completing a field placement at that site during the same semester, facilitating communication and helping to keep the children's interest between visits by the students. Both teams spend time at their site becoming acquainted with the children and teachers, taking photos, and recording children's conversations.

The following week we debrief about that experience. Team A and Team B in each group share their photos and transcripts with each other and try to identify questions the children might have and arrive at a decision about what might make for a worthwhile investigation. They collaborate to brainstorm possibilities and choose a provocation for the next visit. One student from each team takes responsibility for compiling selected photos and narrative into a piece of documentation. The next six weeks could be described as tag-team teaching. Team A brings to the site documentation from the initial visit and the agreed upon materials to serve as provocation for further exploration. Each student has a role. One takes the lead in interacting with the children, revisiting the documentation, and introducing the provocation, another is a photographer and videographer, and the other takes written notes. They return to the college at 11 a.m. to join with their Team B counterparts who have been in the class all morning, discussing issues and questions that have come up through experiences with the children and the reading they have been doing. Together they look at the new photos and discuss the morning's happenings then make decisions about how Team B will proceed when they go to the center the following week. They update me through a weekly journal entry, so I know how they are interpreting encounters with the children and what they intend to do next. I send an e-mail reply prior to the next visit. This continues over the course of six weeks, with Team A and Team B alternating, using documentation as a way to remind the children about what had happened when their counterparts were there the previous week. On each visit, the students rotate roles so each has an opportunity to take the lead interacting, taking photos and videotape, and making written records. Each also takes responsibility for composing one piece of documentation.

The emphasis is on learning, with no expectation of a perfect project. There are challenges associated with the intervals between visits and the alternating teams. This arrangement allows, however, each team between their visits to continue learning more in class about supporting meaningful dialogue with children, composing effective documentation, and understanding other significant aspects of the work involved. At the end of the semester, each group tells the class the story of what they learned, using selected documentation from their experiences with the children and inviting feedback and suggestions about other decisions that could have been made about provocations, questions asked to the children, and ways to document. The students participate in determining the criteria for evaluation guided by the learning outcomes for which we are responsible and also based on what they found to be significant about the experience. They also contribute to evaluating their peers.

How does this process feel for students? This is, after all, a different approach to learning from what many adult students might expect. If you have recently attended college, you will probably remember expecting to listen and learn and prove you have learned. How do we do that? Typically, we do that through tests, papers, and exams. Bringing your own work back to the group for discussion purposes may feel quite daunting, especially if things don't go quite as planned. We know, for example, that children usually have their own ideas about what to do with materials no matter how carefully we have prepared.

A Bridge to Learning

Here is an example of some work by Karyn's students that provided a true learning experience for them, albeit with some disequilibrium involved. Karyn's students experienced many in-depth class discussions about how to observe and reflect and how to provide children with provocations outside of the stereotypes sometimes based on "the interests of the children." When a team of students arrived at their host program quite unprepared in terms of materials and responded to truck play with "transportation" as a focus, there was the risk that a quite superficial experience for the children might occur. But a savvy host teacher saved the day when she gave students time to examine the classroom and think further about their plans.

> The students asked the teacher if there were any plastic boats available to put in the water play bin. The teacher was quite aware of the expectations in the course and wisely replied that she wasn't sure so she would check and, in the meantime, they could look around the room to see if they could generate a back-up plan just in case. She gave them a few minutes before returning with the unfortunate news that there did not seem to be any boats.
>
> In the interim, the students noticed there were numerous pieces of documentation in the classroom about the children's ongoing investigation of bridges. By the time the teacher returned, they had come up with an alternative. The students asked if they could bring the rectangular plastic bin from the water table over to the block area. The teacher happily agreed to this and found towels to place around the bin. They put a few cars on a small mat with roads printed on it at one end of the bin and drew roads on a piece of bristol board to place at the other end. When the children arrived, the students asked them to find a way to get the cars from the roads on the mat to the roads on the bristol board. At first the children flew the cars over, but the students challenged them to find a way real cars (that can't fly) could get over the water. One child, a two-year-old, went to the block shelf and selected the longest block. He attempted to lay it across the bin, which was set lengthwise between the road maps. The bin was longer than the block, and it fell in with a splash. One of the students intervened to turn the bin so the shorter length lay between the roadmaps. The child picked up the block he had retrieved from the water and turned it so it was being placed lengthwise again, with the same outcome. With a bit of prompting, he tried again, laying it across the width of the bin

with success. From there, other children joined in, widening the bridge with more blocks, making ramps, and having a wonderful time driving cars over the bridge. The students returned to class at 11 a.m. jubilant about this experience. They saw a child constructing knowledge. When they shared the video with the class at the end of the semester, they indicated this experience brought home the meaning of "teacher as provocateur." They also shared their recognition of intervening too quickly to turn the bin instead of encouraging collaborative problem-solving. The pressure of being videotaped can lead to a desire to have everything go right, but using the video as a tool for reflection allowed them to identify this to their classmates. They also recognized if there had been boats that day the experience would likely not have been as rich and interesting for the children or for them, even though they could have written a rationale for what the children learned through play with the boats. It would have been predictable, and the children no doubt would have been happily occupied awhile. These students found out much more is possible.

The experience Karyn described here demonstrates beautifully the power and influence of documentation. When others read about and view children's work, the documentation provides a window for them to think about what the children are doing. After reflection, the possibilities for response begin to open up. For these students, a whole new possibility emerged.

The other important factor during this particular practicum experience was the flexibility and openness of the cooperating teacher. With varied materials on hand and an open mind, she was able to support the student teachers through an important pivotal point.

Karyn also explained how educators in her community came together to learn about the power of reflective practice and, in the process, forged powerful relationships that continue to nourish their thinking.

Of course, ours is an ecology of relationships. It would not be feasible to send students out to try to learn about emergent curriculum and to try to interpret the meaning of the Reggio philosophy in a community that is not supportive. In 1998, I started a network of educators in our city who were interested in meeting regularly to share experiences and learning. Two years later, I submitted a proposal to our local community foundation to seek funding for artists who might learn with us and deepen our understanding of aspects of the Reggio Emilia philosophy. This grant allowed us to hire four artists in the spring of 2001. Eight years and many proposals later, we have eight artists in a total of seventeen programs and have had eight annual exhibits of the children's work and accompanying documentation. Our website, www.artistsatthecentre.ca, has examples of documentation and postings of articles that have been published in journals about the project.

Even with these opportunities and supports on many levels, change on a big scale is extremely challenging. It is necessary to create some disequilibrium, some dissatisfaction with the status quo, before there will be an inclination to change. We always do the best we can with what we know. Changing the way we teach can imply what we have been doing is wrong. There can be a strong impetus to stay the course. There are always pressures to conform, to use checklists and prepared packages for behavior guidance and curriculum, rather than questioning the foundation of our practice—our views of children, teaching, and learning. It is unsettling not to know what is coming next and to have to explain to others what we are doing when we may not be entirely sure ourselves. Crossing those borders and learning authentically offers a level of excitement and satisfaction that is transformative. Our opportunities to have encounters with Lella Gandini, Amelia Gambetti, and Carlina Rinaldi (liaison and educators from Reggio Emilia, Italy) and to host The Hundred Languages of Children exhibit from Italy in nearby Toronto have inspired educators who have made the commitment to change. When we can invite others in our community to join us, to challenge us, to learn with us, to try to interpret this complex and rich philosophy in our context, it is much more likely that the change can be sustained. Our souls will be changed.

When instructors work with adult students, especially in college settings where courses are often taught in more traditional ways, it is easy to maintain the status quo. What is more challenging and infinitely more rewarding for everyone is to provide experiences for adult students that are authentic, create opportunities for dialogue, and provoke some disequilibrium—and therefore deep thinking—about the classroom situations in which students find themselves. When such meaningful opportunities exist, instructors are helping to create a group of critical and creative thinkers who will eventually make their mark on our profession.

Educators who are training adults to work with young children and administrators who are mentoring teachers in the workforce have a deep responsibility to think about how curriculum might be developed and how the process of curriculum development might be experienced and examined in authentic ways by adult learners. It is important to provide for professional dialogue on a regular basis and to model reflective and responsive practices either in the workplace or in the college classroom. Instructors and administrators must also be willing to experience some disequilibrium. Only then can they expect teachers of children to be able to approach their work with children in fresh ways, with minds that are open and flexible, and with the disposition of curious researchers who are passionate about children's thinking and ideas.

10

Taking the Leap:
The Unscripted Path

Life is intent on finding what works, not what's "right." It is the ability
to keep finding solutions that is important; any one solution is tem-
porary. There are no permanently right answers. The capacity to keep
changing, to find what works now, is what keeps any organism alive.

—MARGARET J. WHEATLEY AND MYRON KELLNER-ROGERS

You have read in the teachers' stories in this book that emergent curriculum allows
for choices and decision making on the part of both the teacher and the child, which
happens through a collaboration between them. When we factor in the role and
influence of observations, a thoughtfully prepared and rich environment, and our
own and children's questions and ideas, many possibilities become available to us.

While choice is a good thing for both teachers and children, it can be daunting
for teachers who are used to prescribed curricula and for anyone who is completely
new to emergent curriculum. Decision making in an environment in which we can
make creative decisions is exciting as well as challenging. Think back to Naomi's

first journal entries and how she demonstrated that emergent curriculum for the newcomer can be both stimulating and confusing, can create passion and uncertainty. Yet, overall, it allows for huge growth within the teacher.

In this final chapter, an emergent curriculum project that includes all of the factors described in this book is examined. Naomi's very first project is also described, because it was a courageous topic to tackle and it involved innovative ideas. Naomi was required to put previous learning about curricula on hold while she considered many possibilities, none of which she had ever encountered before.

Naomi's Journal

I am beginning to dislike Wednesdays! I am pretty sure that last Wednesday I had the same headache and body ache! I'm stumped about where to proceed from this point in my planning. As I look around the classroom, it seems that only a few children have become fully engaged with the transparency-focused centers during the afternoon. Perhaps the children who aren't engaged do not fully understand how to engage with the materials. Maybe the purpose isn't clear or the invitation isn't inviting enough. Are the materials not sufficiently open-ended? I find it difficult to know what the underlying causes are. Maybe it's as simple as that by pursuing questions of a few pertaining to transparency many others who are uninterested have been caught under the "transparent umbrella" against their will when there are other things on their mind . . . which I could have missed. I don't know.

Tracing the Path of the Transparency Project

In September, when the children were new to school and teachers were attempting to learn more about them, the classroom was arranged with fairly typical materials. Along with ample studio supplies in one area, there were places for construction, reading and writing, exploring items from the natural world, and acting out various experiences.

Naomi was responsible for the afternoon program. As a team, we decided, since four- and five-year-olds are natural explorers of how the world works, we would begin the afternoon program with a focus on science. If approached in broad terms, we hypothesized, we would soon learn through observation and listening what exactly the children were curious about and what their theories were.

At this point in the year, all the children were four years old, except for two younger children. We noticed almost immediately that the three-year-olds had a continuing need for sensory work. They were attracted to it and spent long periods of time—up to an hour—at these centers. Therefore, Naomi arranged for two or three different water centers to be available each afternoon, and these were hugely popular. One of the centers was a large bin with clear vessels for holding water, such as small glass vials and bottles, plastic bags, test tubes, and so on. One boy, Adam, spent several long periods working with these materials. After a few days of pouring and watching, Adam held up his plastic bag full of water toward a light source and proclaimed, "Hey, I can see through this!"

The following day, in response to this comment, clear glass rocks were added to the water, and two children held them up to the ceiling lights. One child commented to the other, "You won't be able to see through a rock!" But, through further experimentation, they found they could indeed see all the way through. Another child filled a glass jar with the same glass rocks and water and said, "You can't see it!"

As the teaching team watched this exploration and noticed the children's confusion about what one could or couldn't see through, it

▲ Children explore water and transparent materials for the first time.

raised questions for us about how much children could understand about transparency.

You have probably noticed children who, when working with transparent materials, hold up an object in order to look through it. It is natural to respond by providing more materials and to interact with the children about what they see. In this case, though, it was the children's comments that provoked our teaching team to ask questions about what the children actually understood. This "habit of listening" is a powerful one when engaging in emergent curriculum. It was during a team discussion about the children's comments that the idea of exploring transparency more deeply began to take shape. Though not a typical topic for young children to explore, it is one we felt would relate directly to what the children were discussing. Their words and actions enabled us to see their thinking, understandings, and misunderstandings.

Simultaneously, other children were building cities in the block area. Naomi wondered if they would be able to map their block cities. To answer her question, she introduced an overhead projector with sheets of acetate to a group of children and they attempted to map the classroom.

It quickly became apparent that the children were much more interested in the overhead projector and the transparent film than in mapping. Many children flocked to the overhead projector on a daily basis. Over the next two weeks, Naomi provided for plentiful experiences with light, shadow, and color, watching for children's understandings and misunderstandings.

▲ Teacher and child explore transparency further with an overhead projector and trays of colored water.

◄ Children explore natural materials on the overhead projector.

▼ During water play, a child explores transparent materials.

◄ A child peers through her drawing produced on acetate.

When watching children in action, it is difficult to know what to respond to. In this case, Naomi was not sure whether to follow up on an intense interest in building complex structures. It is helpful, in such an instance, to acknowledge you have a question that remains unanswered or is puzzling. With this mind-set, it is possible to formulate a question for yourself. The question might be something like "How can I find out if this is worth pursuing?" For Naomi, the invitation to make maps of the cities was one she felt would give her an answer. If the children responded positively to this idea, she would follow them and there would be two investigations (mapping and transparency) going on at the same time. If not, she would simply let go of mapping and the children would continue to build using their own agendas. As the story shows, there was an unexpected response to her invitation that actually tied in to the ongoing investigation of transparency.

The teacher is *responsive* in that she provides for many choices and time to experiment. Time is such an important aspect of emergent curriculum. As discussed earlier, we all need time to absorb new information, to use it in playful and experimental ways, to try things over and over again, and to develop methods of describing what we've discovered. This is true of both adults and children. Giving children time—in this case weeks—to experiment with a new piece of equipment, which in turn helps to solidify their understanding of a new concept, is crucial if we are going to truly understand their thinking and know what to do next. The teacher needs time, too, to listen carefully and to think about what is unfolding.

> The children explored freely with the overhead projector every afternoon using many kinds of opaque, translucent, and transparent materials. They also used everyday classroom materials and sorted them into categories based on which ones projected color or shadow or no color or shadow. Naomi noticed during this time that children had reached a "cognitive knot," meaning they sometimes confused "clear" with "white" and also believed something could not be colored and transparent at the same time.

Notice in this journal entry that, although Naomi recognized a knot in the children's thinking, she did not hurry in with the answer. She realized it is more helpful to scaffold children's learning by providing supports and materials that will allow the children to reach their own understanding.

It was at this point that the team decided we needed a taped conversation with the children in order to better understand their thinking. For the children, this conversation solidified how to articulate what they already knew, and for Naomi it made clearer how to move the exploration forward. This series of conversations took several days, and it took Naomi a long time to transcribe it.

To assist the children with distinguishing between *clear* and *white*, they were invited to draw on both white paper and transparent film. Some of them learned how to trace their paper drawings, and others were able to see their transparent drawings on the overhead projector.

The teaching team spiraled back to dialogue and reflection, which happens over and over again during projects and investigations. This kind of touching base, reflection, idea sharing, and collaborative decision making is an important aspect of emergent curriculum and needs to be included on a regular basis in our teaching lives. Direct response to children's confusion is an attempt to clarify a difficult concept for them. It comes in the form of another invitation that allows the children to construct their own knowledge.

After the team reflected on the taped discussions, Naomi felt the children understood the term *transparent* and decided to introduce the connected and yet different term *invisible* to them to see what they made of it. Together, they read *The Emperor's New Clothes*. Then the children made a portrait of themselves on white paper and traced it onto overhead transparencies.

The teacher asked the children, "What would you look or feel like if you were see-through or invisible?" The children explained what it would look or feel like, and their words were written on the transparencies:

- If I was invisible, my dad would be invisible and my grandmother couldn't see my eyes.

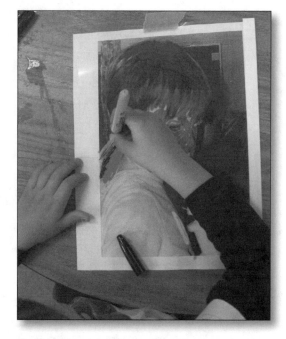

▲ A black and white photo is covered with acetate so that a child can draw over the top of it or add blocks of color to it.

- If I was invisible, I would bump into things.
- If I was invisible, it would feel like I was flying.
- If I was invisible, it would be like I was floating through the air.

It took several weeks and a great variety of materials to explore before the children solidified their understandings of the words *clear, transparent, see-through,* and *invisible.* When they began to understand these terms, we wondered if the children could use transparent film as a tool throughout the classroom over the long term, just as they use pencils, paint, and glue. The acetate was placed in the studio area for their continued use, while we watched, waited, and wondered how the children and teachers would use this new material as a tool for further learning.

The children have time to solidify their understandings before moving on. As they move on to other projects and investigations unrelated to transparency, the transparent acetate, an important part of their investigation, remains in the studio, becoming part of their repertoire of materials to be revisited as needed.

Naomi's Journal

When I think back to the way I used to teach lessons and assess, I'm wondering if the children really understood or were merely able to recite back what it was that they knew I wanted to hear. So many times, I wondered why there was so much difficulty with the lack of depth in their understanding and the ability to think outside of the box, or hypothesize and infer. Could it be because I was telling them what they needed to learn and not allowing them to wonder, be curious, and explore for themselves? I don't think that even once I asked myself to step back and see what it was that they really understood instead of what they could do. Reflection requires looking backwards, and teaching is a never-ending journey of pressing onward.

At the end of the day, when all the teachers and children have gone home, I am left alone with my notes and empty planning sheets and my inexperience with emergent curriculum (and with teaching in general). I feel like a stranger surrounded by a foreign language, and I am the only one who doesn't understand

it. Where is the fine line between creating an environment that supports learn-
ing with its richness of materials and opportunities for independent exploration
and an environment that is too constructed, to the point where it is no longer
open-ended and inquiry-based . . . an environment where I've stormed in
with my need to plan and be prepared and set everything up so carefully that
I've accidentally done all the work for them, so there is no need to think and
wonder? (Gasp for air!)

Wow! I am feeling excited. If I'm remembering the term correctly, I think I
observed (and actually noticed—as I've come to see that they are two differ-
ent things) an example of a cognitive knot. When using different paper-like
materials to explore transparency, J. called the overhead transparency "white"
when I asked what color it was. I then showed him a piece of white paper and
asked him what color it was, and he again said "white." All of a sudden, confu-
sion spread over his face as he looked from the transparency to the paper. It was
clear that he could tell there was a difference between the two, but he either had
no words to use or no understanding of what "clear" meant.

POSTSCRIPT

Two months after the children explored transparency, they became immersed in a
study of the human body, and they showed particular interest in what is inside the
body. Since many children came from families who work in medical professions,
they had a great deal of prior knowledge on this topic. They used correct terminol-
ogy for organs, knew the functions of many of them, and could represent the inside
of the human body with accuracy.

While reading a book about the human body, one term confused the children.
They did not seem to understand what a cast was for, even though they had seen
people wearing them. During a team meeting, the teachers wondered, "Can the
children's use of transparent acetates enable them to show what they think is going
on inside the cast?"

Here was an opportunity to spiral back to the idea of transparency and use it
as a tool for understanding another topic. The teachers raised their own questions,
thereby engaging in *collaboration* as the curriculum unfolded. Then they engaged in

brainstorming another invitation to support the children's quest to understand casts. This is a perfect example of the back and forth nature of emergent curriculum. A question arises from the children, which results in reflection and brainstorming on the part of the teachers, who provide the children with further investigations.

After a conversation about broken bones, an invitation was set up in the studio. Could the children use acetate as well as regular paper to figure out what was going on inside and outside a cast? Here are the results of their thinking.

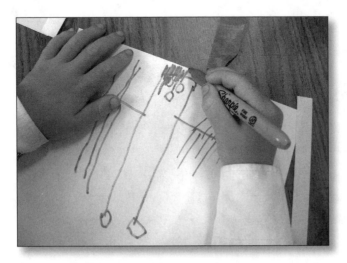

▲ The original drawing is made on paper.

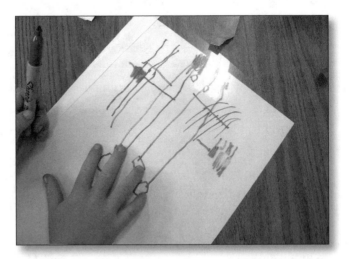

▲ Another drawing is made on acetate and placed on top of the original. The child now has an understanding of what's going on inside and outside the cast.

This investigation of transparency shows that interesting and thought-provoking curriculum can emerge from simple beginnings. In this case, a child noticing that he can see through water led to questions for the teacher, who provided some invitations for the children, and the cycle continues.

Naomi's Journal

This week I reached the point where I wasn't sure what to do next in my planning. After talking with my colleagues, I was reminded that whenever I reach this point I need to go straight to the source . . . the children. If I was using a premade curriculum, I would consult my outcome guide or my unit overview, but with emergent curriculum, the children are the source of inspiration. After being reminded of that, I began asking more prompting questions and looking more closely for any misunderstandings the children might have.

Conclusion

When developing curricula, it is the teacher's attentiveness to details that opens up possibilities for exploration. In a classroom that uses emergent curriculum, watching and listening for small details becomes second nature. Teachers begin to gather so much data—on paper, with photos, or in their memories—that there is a wealth of information to discuss and possibly act on. When we create many possibilities, there is more of a chance that something innovative, creative, and unexpected will emerge in response. It is in this way, through exploring the unexpected and putting the teacher in the role of researcher, that curricula for young children can move forward and teachers and children can find or rediscover their passion for learning.

When you return to your classroom after reading and thinking about emergent curriculum, try to see the environment, equipment, and, most of all, the children and their ideas through new eyes.

Allow yourself to dream. When you allow yourself to imagine what might be, without censorship or logic, you open your mind, giving creativity a chance to flourish.

Engage in talking with others. Don't keep your dreams, thoughts, and ideas to yourself. When you share your thoughts with other educators, artists, and professionals, you multiply your chances of developing new approaches to your teaching practice. Work at finding a way to have discussions on a regular basis. They don't cost anything, and the possibilities are endless.

Become comfortable with disequilibrium. When you begin considering new approaches to anything in your adult life, it is common to feel anxious. When you recognize that disequilibrium can be a positive force, you can learn to embrace it and even enjoy it.

Seek out supports or support others. Everyone going through a period of professional and creative growth needs a cheerleader—someone who is encouraging, a good listener, and a provocateur who asks difficult and thought-provoking questions. Find a person whom you will support and a person who will support you.

Recognize your successes, no matter how small. Wonderful things begin with small changes. Recognize these as significant. Celebrate and talk about them with colleagues and families.

Early childhood curriculum is tremendously important and needs to be treated seriously by society. By bringing cutting-edge curricula to the attention of those both inside and outside our field, we can move our profession onward and upward.

When thinking with children during investigations and collaborating with them in the journey of learning, we rediscover what children already know and are willing to teach us: humans are creative by nature. When we watch, listen, and experience new things with pleasure and true curiosity and then respond by trusting our prior knowledge and intuition, a truly engaging curriculum emerges.

Appendix:
Blank Observation
and Planning Forms

Observation	Teacher's Reflection	Response: Invitations, Conversations, Activities, Projects	Follow-up Observation

Classroom area: _____

Week of: _____

Observer: _____

Monday	Tuesday	Wednesday	Thursday	Friday
Responses / Plans	*Responses / Plans*	*Responses / Plans*	*Responses / Plans*	*Responses / Plans*
Observations	*Observations*	*Observations*	*Observations*	*Observations*

Bibliography

Carter, Margie, and Deb Curtis. 1994. *The Art of Awareness: How Observation Can Transform Your Teaching*. St. Paul: Redleaf Press.

———. 1994. *Training Teachers: A Harvest of Theory and Practice*. St. Paul: Redleaf Press.

Copple, Carol, and Sue Bredekamp, eds. 2009. *Developmentally Appropriate Practice in Early Childhood Programs Serving Children from Birth through Age 8*. 3rd ed. Washington, DC: National Association for the Education of Young Children.

Csikszentmihalyi, Mihaly. 1990. *Flow: The Psychology of Optimal Experience*. New York: HarperCollins Publishers.

———. 1996. *Creativity: Flow and the Psychology of Discovery and Invention*. New York: HarperCollins Publishers.

Dittman, Laura, ed. 1970. *Curriculum Is What Happens*. Washington, DC: National Association for the Education of Young Children.

Duckworth, Eleanor. 2006. *"The Having of Wonderful Ideas" and Other Essays on Teaching and Learning*. 3rd ed. New York: Teachers College Press.

Fraser, Susan, and Carol Gestwicki. 2002. *Authentic Childhood: Experiencing Reggio Emilia in the Classroom*. Albany: Delmar.

Gandini, Lella, and Carolyn Pope Edwards, eds. 2001. *Bambini: The Italian Approach to Infant/Toddler Care*. New York: Teachers College Press.

Goldsworthy, Andy. 1990. *Andy Goldsworthy: A Collaboration with Nature*. New York: Harry N. Abrams.

Goleman, Daniel, Paul Kaufman, and Michael Ray. 1992. *The Creative Spirit*. New York: Penguin Books.

Helm, Judy Harris, and Lilian Katz. 2001. *Young Investigators: The Project Approach in the Early Years*. New York: Teachers College Press.

Hill, Lynn T., Andrew J. Stremmel, and Victoria R. Fu. 2005. *Teaching as Inquiry: Rethinking Curriculum in Early Childhood Education*. Boston: Pearson/Allyn & Bacon.

Jones, Elizabeth. 1993. *Growing Teachers: Partnerships in Staff Development*. Washington, DC: National Association for the Education of Young Children.

Jones, Elizabeth. 2007. *Teaching Adults, Revisited: Active Learning for Early Childhood Educators*. Washington, DC: National Association for the Education of Young Children.

Jones, Elizabeth, and Renatta M. Cooper. 2006. *Playing to Get Smart*. New York: Teachers College Press.

Jones, Elizabeth, and John Nimmo. 1994. *Emergent Curriculum*. Washington, DC: National Association for the Education of Young Children.

Kaminsky, Judith Allen, and Lella Gandini. 2005. "The Challenge of Diversity: An Interview with Carol Brunson Day and Margie Carter." *Innovations in Early Education* 12 (4): 17–23.

Kaulbach, Kathy. 2010. Personal correspondence with author.

Keeler, Rusty. 2008. *Natural Playscapes: Creating Outdoor Play Environments for the Soul.* Redmond, WA: Exchange Press.

Kinney, Linda, and Pat Wharton. 2008. *An Encounter with Reggio Emilia: Children's Early Learning Made Visible.* New York: Routledge.

Louv, Richard. 2008. *Last Child in the Woods: Saving Our Children from Nature-Deficit Disorder.* Chapel Hill: Algonquin Books of Chapel Hill.

Palmer, Parker J. 1998. *The Courage to Teach: Exploring the Inner Landscape of a Teacher's Life.* San Francisco: Jossey-Bass.

Project Zero. 2003. *Making Teaching Visible: Documenting Individual and Group Learning as Professional Development.* Cambridge: Harvard University Graduate School of Education.

Rinaldi, Carlina. 2006. *In Dialogue with Reggio Emilia: Listening, Researching and Learning.* New York: Routledge.

Robinson, Ken, with Lou Aronica. 2009. *The Element: How Finding Your Passion Changes Everything.* New York: Viking.

Stacey, Susan. 2009. *Emergent Curriculum in Early Childhood Settings: From Theory to Practice.* St. Paul: Redleaf Press.

Von Oech, Roger. 2002. *Expect the Unexpected or You Won't Find It: A Creativity Tool Based on the Ancient Wisdom of Heraclitus.* San Francisco: Berrett-Koehler Publishers.

Wheatley, Margaret J., and Myron Kellner-Rogers. 1999. *A Simpler Way.* San Francisco, CA: Berrett-Koehler Publishers.

Wien, Carol Anne, and Susan Kirby-Smith. 1998. "Untiming the Curriculum: A Case Study of Removing Clocks from the Program." *Young Children* 53 (5): 8–13.

Wien, Carol Anne, ed. 2008. *Emergent Curriculum in the Primary Classroom: Interpreting the Reggio Emilia Approach in Schools.* New York: Teachers College Press.

Photography Credits

Photographs on page 42 by Anne Marie Coughlin

Photographs on pages 81–82 by Andrea Foster

Photographs on pages 58–62 by Susan Hagner

Photographs on pages 84–85 by Shannon Harrison

Photographs on page 24 (top) by Elizabeth Hicks

Photographs on pages 29 and 31–32 by Lana O'Reilly

Photographs on pages 24 (bottom) and 49–51 by Melissa Pinkham

Photographs on pages 121–22, 123 (right), and 125 by Naomi Robinson

Photographs on pages 73–77 by Liz Rogers

Photographs on pages 11, 14, 23, 26, 98–101, 123 (top left and bottom left), and 128 by Susan Stacey

Photographs on page 64 by Michelle Tessier

Photograph on page 107 by Lori Warner